Houghton Mifflin
Mathematics

Reteach

5

HOUGHTON MIFFLIN

BOSTON • MORRIS PLAINS, NJ

California • Colorado • Georgia • Illinois • New Jersey • Texas

Contents

Name _____   Date _____

Place Value to Hundred Thousands

You can read and write numbers in different ways.

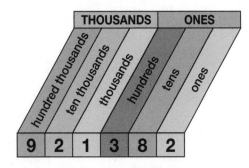

You can use **standard form.**	921,382
You can use **expanded form.**	$(9 \times 100{,}000) + (2 \times 10{,}000) +$ $(1 \times 1{,}000) + (3 \times 100) + (8 \times 10) +$ (2×1)
You can use **word form.**	nine hundred twenty-one thousand, three hundred eighty-two
You can use **short word form.**	921 thousand, 382

Write each number in word form and in expanded form.

1. 83,903

_____

_____

_____

2. 98,340

_____

_____

_____

3. 489,341

_____

_____

_____

4. 398,473

_____

_____

_____

Name _____ Date _____

Exponents

A short way to write $10 \times 10 \times 10 \times 10$ is 10^4. When you read 10^4, say "ten to the fourth power." The 10 is the **base**. The small raised 4 is the **exponent**.

THOUSANDS			ONES		
hundred thousands	ten thousands	thousands	hundreds	tens	ones
100,000	10,000	1,000	100	10	1
$10\times10\times10\times10\times10$	$10\times10\times10\times10$	$10\times10\times10$	10×10	10	1
10^5	10^4	10^3	10^2	10^1	10^0

This place-value chart shows each place as a **power of ten**. You can use powers of ten when you write numbers in expanded form.

Different ways to write 981,248:	
You can use **expanded form**:	$(9 \times 100{,}000) + (8 \times 10{,}000) + (1 \times 1{,}000) +$ $(2 \times 100) + (4 \times 10) + (8 \times 1)$
You can use **expanded form with exponents**:	$(9 \times 10^5) + (8 \times 10^4) + (1 \times 10^3) + (2 \times 10^2) +$ $(4 \times 10^1) + (8 \times 10^0)$

Write each number in expanded form with exponents.

1. 8,394 _____

2. 93,842 _____

3. 98,347 _____

4. 19,302 _____

5. 853,403 _____

6. 173,284 _____

7. 557,392 _____

Name _____ Date _____

Compare, Order, and Round Whole Numbers

Compare the numbers 94,304 and 94,871.

| **Step 1** Line up the numbers by place value. | 9 4 3 0 4
 9 4 8 7 1 | **Step 2** Start from the left. Compare the digits until they are different. | 9 4 **3** 0 4
 9 4 **8** 7 1 | The hundreds digit, 3, is less than 8, so 94,308 < 94,871 |

Compare. Write >, <, or = for each ◯.

1. 83,204 ◯ 87,204
2. 192,932 ◯ 93,204
3. 8,922 ◯ 8,927

Use rounding rules to round 873,485 to the nearest hundred thousand.

Step 1 Circle the place you want to round to.	**Step 2** Look at the digit to its right.	**Step 3** If that digit is 5 or greater, increase the rounding place digit by 1. If that digit is less than 5, do not change the rounding place digit. Then replace all digits to the right with zeros.
⑧73,485 rounding place	873,485 digit to the right	873,485 ↓ 900,000 7 > 5 Change 8 to 9. Write zeros to the right.

Round to the place of the underlined digit.

4. 85,204 _____
5. 933,418 _____
6. 682,395 _____

Order from greatest to least.   9,475   8,338   8,358

Line up the digits.   9 4 7 5 ← greatest number
Compare from the left.   8 3 3 8 ← least number
Continue comparing.   8 3 5 8   9,475 > 8,358 > 8,338

Order these numbers from greatest to least.

7. 35,829; 48,204; 38,205 _____
8. 933,273; 938,273; 827,478 _____

Name _____ Date _____

Problem-Solving Skill: Estimated or Exact Answers

We use an estimate for an amount that cannot be measured easily. An amount that has been rounded is an estimate.

Tammy is making gingerbread cookies for the school fair. She knows that there will be several hundred people at the fair and hopes that each of them will want at least 2 cookies. Each recipe of frosting that she makes will frost exactly 20 gingerbread cookies. Her recipes call for 3 pounds of sugar and more than 5 pounds of flour. She can spend no more than $20.00 on all the ingredients. She plans to sell the cookies for $0.50 each and hopes to sell over 400 of them.

Decide if an amount if estimated or exact.

1. There will be several hundred people at the fair.

   Think: What word will tell you whether the amount is estimated or exact?

   _____

2. Tammy hopes each person will want at least 2 gingerbread cookies.

   Think: What word will tell you whether the amount is estimated or exact?

   _____

3. Each recipe of frosting will frost 20 gingerbread cookies.

   Think: Which amounts have been counted or measured?

   _____

4. Her recipe calls for 3 pounds of sugar.

   Think: Which amounts have been counted or measured?

   _____

5. She will use more than 5 pounds of flour.

   Think: What word will tell you whether the amount is estimated or exact?

   _____

6. Tammy will sell the gingerbread cookies for $0.50.

   Think: Which amounts have been counted or measured?

   _____

Name _____ Date _____

Millions and Billions

Different Ways to Read and Write Numbers:	
You can use **standard form:**	8,467,374,219
You can use **expanded form:**	$(8 \times 1,000,000,000) + (4 \times 100,000,000) +$ $(6 \times 10,000,000) + (7 \times 1,000,000) +$ $(3 \times 100,000) + (7 \times 10,000) + (4 \times 1,000) +$ $(2 \times 100) + (1 \times 10) + (9 \times 1)$
You can use **expanded word form with exponents:**	$(8 \times 10^9) + (4 \times 10^8) + (6 \times 10^7) + (7 \times 10^6) +$ $(3 \times 10^5) + (7 \times 10^4) + (4 \times 10^3) + (2 \times 10^2) +$ $(1 \times 10^1) + (9 \times 10^0)$
You can use **short word form:**	8 billion, 467 million, 374 thousand, 219
You can use **word form:**	eight billion, four hundred sixty-seven million, three hundred seventy-four thousand, two hundred nineteen

Write the numbers in short word form, expanded form, and expanded form using exponents.

1. 873,485,309

_____

_____

_____

_____

2. 94,305,394,471

_____

_____

_____

_____

Order each set of numbers from greatest to least.

3. 683,573,484   68,324,204   868,204,482 _____

4. 1,302,475,328   83,294,273   483,274,284 _____

Name _____ Date _____

Round Large Numbers

Round 638,302,402 to the nearest million.

You can use rounding rules.

Step 1 Find the millions place.	**Step 2** Use rounding rules.
638,302,402	3 < 5
Find the digit to its right.	8 does not change.
638,302,402	638,000,000

Round each number to the nearest million.

1. 4,586,477

2. 9,824,382

3. 475,438,202

4. 7,577,456,235

5. 399,448,981,338

6. 45,205,249,472

7. 58,403,284

8. 372,374,119,301

9. 48,937,940

Round the number to the nearest billion.

10. 51,849,513,575

11. 548,843,519,846

12. 35,518,641,000

13. 51,999,218,275

14. 88,451,328,849

15. 8,124,943,205

16. 84,849,475,204

17. 351,103,483,578

18. 983,284,292,458

Name _____ Date _____

Problem-Solving Strategy: Guess and Check

Sometimes, the quickest way to solve a problem is to check a few numbers to see if they work.

> Oscar is thinking of a number between 15 and 30. His number is divisible by 3 and 4. What number is Oscar thinking about?

Understand *What is the question?* Find the number.

What do you know? It is greater than 15 and less than 30. It can be divided by 3 and 4.

Plan *How can you find the answer?* Guess and Check to find the number.

Solve

| Guess: 18 | Check: 18 ÷ 3 = 6; 18 ÷ 4 = 4 R2 | 18 is divisible by 3, but not by 4. |
| Guess: 24 | Check: 24 ÷ 3 = 8; 24 ÷ 4 = 6 | 24 is divisible by both 3 and 4. |

Solution: The number is 24.

Look Back Check to make sure that 24 fits the information in the problem.

Solve each problem using the Guess and Check strategy.

1. Wally has 30 fish in his tank. There are twice as many goldfish as guppies. How many goldfish are there? How many guppies?

   Think: What information should you start with?

   _____

2. Nick's wallet contains 6 bills. He has only $1.00 and $10.00 bills and has a total of $42.00. What combination of bills does he have?

   Think: What types of bills are in Nick's wallet?

   _____

3. Paulo is thinking of a number between 1 and 10. When you double the number and add 3, you get 11. Find the number Paulo is thinking of.

   Think: What information should you start with?

   _____

4. Lazaro and his father have a combined height of 105 inches. If Lazaro's father is twice Lazaro's height, how tall is Lazaro? his father?

   Think: What information should you start with?

   _____

Name _____ Date _____

Place Value and Decimals

Use the place-value chart to understand decimals.

The value of digits to the right
of the decimal point is less than one.

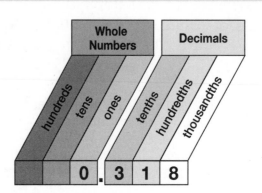

Standard form: 0.318

Word form: three hundred eighteen thousandths

Write each decimal in words.

1. 5.9

_____

_____

2. 9.3

_____

_____

3. 0.24

_____

_____

4. 0.93

_____

_____

5. 0.048

_____

_____

6. 0.081

_____

_____

7. 5.982

_____

_____

8. 4.204

_____

_____

9. 2.092

_____

_____

10. 79.239

_____

_____

_____

11. 475.29

_____

_____

_____

12. 8,345.547

_____

_____

_____

Name _____   Date _____

Compare and Order Decimals Less than One

Which number is greater? Compare 0.3 and 0.25.

Different Ways to Compare Decimals

You can use a number line.

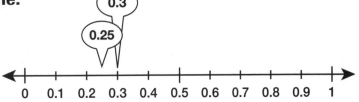

0.3 is to the right of 0.25,
so 0.3 > 0.25

You can compare digits.

Line up the decimal points. Compare digits until they are different.
Since 3 > 2, 0.3 > 0.25

Solution: 0.3 is greater than 0.25.

Compare the decimals. Write >, <, or = for each ◯.

1. 0.45 ◯ 0.48

2. 0.8 ◯ 0.09

3. 0.87 ◯ 0.870

4. 0.448 ◯ 0.488

5. 0.58 ◯ 0.093

6. 0.33 ◯ 0.033

Order each set of numbers from least to greatest.

7. 0.09   0.9   0.3

8. 0.33   0.44   0.28

_____

_____

9. 0.38   0.28   0.478

10. 0.51   0.511   0.522   0.508

_____

_____

Name _____   Date _____

Round Decimals

Round 0.587 to the nearest hundredth.

Different Ways to Round Decimals

You can use a number line.

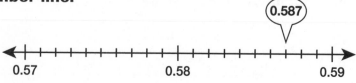

0.587

0.57   0.58   0.59

Decide whether 0.587 is closer to 0.58 or 0.59.

You can use rounding rules.

Step 1 Find the place you want to round to.	**Step 2** Look at the digit to the right.	**Step 3** Round.
0.587 ↑ rounding place	0.587 ↑ digit to the right	0.587 7 > 5 ↓ 0.59 Change 8 to 9.

Solution: The decimal 0.587 rounded to the nearest hundredth is 0.59.

Use a number line to round to the place value of the underlined digit.

1. 0.248

_____

2. 0.827

_____

3. 0.38

_____

4. 0.837

_____

5. 0.583

_____

6. 0.8372

_____

7. 0.264

_____

8. 12.2163

_____

9. 22.2217

_____

10. 8.293

_____

11. 9.8001

_____

12. 6.2942

_____

Name _____ Date _____

Compare and Order Decimals and Whole Numbers

Compare 42.37 and 42.71.

Different Ways to Compare Decimals

You can use a number line.

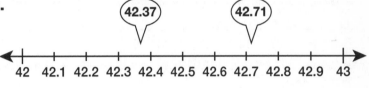

Since 42.37 is to the left of 42.71 on the number line, 42.37 < 42.71

You can compare digits.

Step 1 Line up the decimal points.	**Step 2** Starting from the left, compare digits until they are different.
42.37 42.71	Since 3 < 7, 42.37 < 42.71

Solution: 42.37 is less than 42.71.

Compare. Write >, <, or = for each ◯.

1. 1 ◯ 0.251

2. 8.3 ◯ 0.928

3. 4.382 ◯ 3.402

4. 9.38 ◯ 9.380

5. 83 ◯ 109.384

6. 4.389 ◯ 4.34

Order each set of numbers from least to greatest.

7. 8   0.89   0.38

_____

8. 9.0   0.9   9.99

_____

9. 0.87   0.78   0.788   0.877

_____

10. 6   4.6   8.3   2.99

_____

Name _____   Date _____

Negative Numbers and the Number Line

Compare. 4.5 ◯ ⁻3

Step 1 Locate 4.5 and -3 on the number line.	Step 2 Compare. The number farther left is least and the number farthest right is greatest. Write >, <, or =.

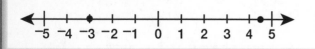

4.5 > ⁻3

Compare. Draw a number line from ⁻5.5 to 5.5 and label every 0.5 unit. Write >, <, or = for each ◯.

⟵————————————————————————————⟶

1. ⁻2 ◯ 3

2. 4 ◯ ⁻2

3. ⁻1 ◯ ⁻2

4. 0 ◯ ⁻3

5. 3 ◯ ⁻4

6. ⁻2 ◯ ⁻2

7. ⁻4.5 ◯ ⁻4.5

8. ⁻0.5 ◯ ⁻4.5

9. 2.5 ◯ ⁻3.5

10. 5 ◯ 2.5

11. 1.5 ◯ 4.5

12. ⁻0.5 ◯ ⁻2

13. ⁻2.5 ◯ ⁻3

14. ⁻3 ◯ 3.5

15. ⁻3.5 ◯ ⁻3.5

Name _____ Date _____

Problem-Solving Application: Use a Table

Marlene is filling bags with party favors for her birthday party. She puts bubbles, gum, and stickers into each bag. Next, she puts two surprise items into each bag: lollipop, jacks, marbles, and sidewalk chalk. How many different combinations of two surprise items are there?

Understand *What is the question?* How many different combinations of two party favors are possible?

Plan *How can you find the answer?* Start with what you know. Make a table to organize the information.

Lollipop	Jacks	Marbles	Sidewalk Chalk
X	X		
X		X	
X			X
	X	X	
	X		X
		X	X

Solve Use an X to show each combination of two different party favors.

There are 6 different combinations of 2 surprise items.

Look Back Look back at the problem. Does your answer make sense?

Make and use a table to solve each problem.

1. Juan is packing his backpack before a hiking trip. He can only fit two of these five items: sunblock; first-aid spray; extra socks; camera; and flashlight. In how many ways can he pack his backpack with two of these items?

   Think: How many combinations of two items are there?

2. The Blast soccer team is traveling to a tournament in cars and vans. Each car holds 4 people and each van holds 6 people. If 5 vehicles are used to transport 24 people, how many of each type of vehicle was used?

   Think: What is a reasonable number of vehicles to carry 24 people?

Name _____   Date _____

Add Whole Numbers

Find 7,492 + 3,158.

Step 1 Add the ones.	**Step 2** Add the tens.	**Step 3** Add the hundreds.	**Step 4** Add the thousands.
Regroup 10 ones as 1 ten if you can. 10 ones = 1 ten 0 ones	Regroup 10 tens as 1 hundred if you can. 14 tens = 1 hundred 4 tens	Regroup 10 hundreds as 1 thousand if you can.	If necessary, also write the ten thousands digit in the sum.
¹ 7,492 +3,158 ⎯⎯ 0	¹¹ 7,492 +3,158 ⎯⎯ 40	¹¹ 7,492 +3,158 ⎯⎯ 640	¹¹ 7,492 +3,158 ⎯⎯ 10,640

Add. Estimate to check that your answer is reasonable.

1. 345 +705
2. 289 +603
3. 387 +640
4. 197 +531
5. 462 +954

6. 6,581 +3,959
7. 3,274 +4,126
8. 6,993 +2,426
9. 645 +4,442
10. 1,785 +6,426

11. 8,113 +5,652
12. 1,455 +5,891
13. 61,422 +13,136
14. 155,540 + 81,612
15. 320,540 +414,228

Name _____ Date _____

Subtract Whole Numbers

Find 3,951 − 1,384.

Step 1 Subtract the ones.	**Step 2** Subtract the tens.	**Step 3** Subtract the hundreds.	**Step 4** Subtract the thousands.
Since 4 > 1 you must regroup 1 ten as 10 ones. 4 11 3,951 −1,384 7	Since 8 > 4 regroup 1 hundred as 10 tens. 14 8 4 11 3,951 −1,384 67	14 8 4 11 3,951 −1,384 567	14 8 4 11 3,951 −1,384 2,567

Subtract. Add to check your answer.

1. 653 − 447
2. 617 − 32
3. 875 − 804
4. 940 − 365
5. 649 − 167

6. 7,032 − 3,792
7. 4,422 − 1,505
8. 4,579 − 2,176
9. 16,197 − 7,920
10. 9,983 − 7,435

11. 8,178 − 723
12. 47,564 − 25,414
13. 50,106 − 20,333

Name _____ Date _____

Problem-Solving Skill: Too Much or Too Little Information

When a problem gives more information than you need, you must decide which information is important. When a problem does not give enough information, you must decide what information is missing.

During the first week of the county fair, 1,544 people rode the Ferris wheel. Out of those 1,544 people, 208 were men, 420 were women, and the rest were children. On Saturday, the busiest day of the fair, 820 people rode the Ferris wheel.

Sometimes you have too much information.
How many children rode the Ferris wheel the first week?

What facts do I need?
- the total number of people who rode the Ferris wheel (1,544)
- the number of men (208) and the number of women (420) who rode the Ferris wheel.

There is additional information provided, but I don't need it.

How can I solve the problem?
- Find the total number of adults who rode the Ferris wheel the first week. 208 + 420 = 628
- Subtract this from the total number of people who rode the Ferris wheel the first week.
  1,544 − 628 = 916 children

Solve each if you can. If a problem is incomplete, tell what information you would need to solve it.

1. There were 1,230 people at the fair on Monday, 828 people on Tuesday and 1,459 people on Saturday. Over 6,000 people attended the fair that week. How many people were at the fair Thursday?

   Think: Is there too much or too little information?

   _____

   _____

   _____

2. A vendor sold balloons for $1.00 and T-shirts for $10.00. He made $1,020 from T-shirts sales and made a total of $1,188 from T-shirt and balloon sales. How many balloons did he sell?

   Think: What information is needed? Do you subtract or add?

   _____

   _____

   _____

Name _____   Date _____

Add Decimals

Find 6.92 + 3.43.

Step 1 Write the addends so digits with the same place value align (line up).	**Step 2** Add the tenths.	**Step 3** Add the ones.
Use the decimal point as a guide. Then, add the hundredths.	Regroup 13 tenths as 1 one and 3 tenths.	Put a decimal point in the sum so it lines up with the decimal points in the addends.
6.92 +3.43 ‾‾‾‾ 5	¹ 6.92 +3.43 ‾‾‾‾ 35	¹ 6.92 +3.43 ‾‾‾‾ 10.35

Find each sum. Estimate to check that your answer is reasonable.

1. 455.21
    +   2.3

2. 79.10
    + 1.925

3. 32.911
    + 0.988

4. $97.23
    + 51.89

5. 8.674
    +32.1

6. 804.54
    + 21.516

7. 11.57
    +0.783

8. 258.41
    +393.66

9. 974.5
    + 90.7

10. 764.4
     +   44.888

11. 42.681 + 2.108

12. 886.32 + 860.41

13. 258.6 + 5.85

_____   _____   _____

Name _____   Date _____

Subtract Decimals

Find 56.21 − 15.35.

Step 1 Write the numbers so digits with the same place value align. Subtract the hundredths.	**Step 2** Subtract the tenths.	**Step 3** Subtract the ones. Write the decimal point in the answer.	**Step 4** Subtract the tens.
$$\begin{array}{r} {}^{1\,11} \\ 56.2\!\!\not\!1 \\ -15.35 \\ \hline 6 \end{array}$$	$$\begin{array}{r} {}^{11} \\ 5\!\!\not\!1\,11 \\ 56.2\!\!\not\!1 \\ -15.35 \\ \hline 86 \end{array}$$	$$\begin{array}{r} {}^{11} \\ 5\!\!\not\!1\,11 \\ 56.2\!\!\not\!1 \\ -15.35 \\ \hline 0.86 \end{array}$$	$$\begin{array}{r} {}^{11} \\ 5\!\!\not\!1\,11 \\ 56.2\!\!\not\!1 \\ -15.35 \\ \hline 40.86 \end{array}$$
You need to regroup 2 tenths as 1 tenth 10 hundredths.	You need to regroup 6 ones as 5 ones and 10 tenths.		

Subtract. Add to check your answer.

1.
$$\begin{array}{r} 8.74 \\ -3.47 \\ \hline \end{array}$$

2.
$$\begin{array}{r} 7.12 \\ -6.16 \\ \hline \end{array}$$

3.
$$\begin{array}{r} \$15.51 \\ -\ \ 4.38 \\ \hline \end{array}$$

4.
$$\begin{array}{r} 28.74 \\ -14.97 \\ \hline \end{array}$$

5.
$$\begin{array}{r} 42.52 \\ -25.66 \\ \hline \end{array}$$

6.
$$\begin{array}{r} 28.12 \\ -\ \ 3.04 \\ \hline \end{array}$$

7.
$$\begin{array}{r} \$71.13 \\ -\ 33.09 \\ \hline \end{array}$$

8.
$$\begin{array}{r} 56.94 \\ -\ \ 9.61 \\ \hline \end{array}$$

9.
$$\begin{array}{r} 45.02 \\ -38.22 \\ \hline \end{array}$$

10.
$$\begin{array}{r} 62.42 \\ -24.44 \\ \hline \end{array}$$

11. 6.45 − 3.87

12. 17.85 − 12.12

13. 81.61 − 61.24

Name _____   Date _____

Problem-Solving Strategy: Work Backward

Sometimes you can start with what you know in a problem and work backward.

PROBLEM At a track-and-field meet, the winning team of the relay race won in 10.54 minutes. This was 0.46 minutes faster than the second-place team. The second-place team ran the race 1.20 minutes faster than the third-place team. How long did it take the third-place team to finish the relay race?

Understand What is the question?

How long did it take the third-place team to finish the relay race?

Solve Start with the 10.54 minute time set by the winner.

First Place	Second Place	Third Place
10.54 minutes	$10.54 - 0.46 = 10.08$	$10.08 - 1.20 = 8.88$
This was 0.46 minutes faster than the second-place time.	The second–place time was 1.20 minutes faster than the third–place time.	The third–place time was 8.88 minutes

---

Solve each problem using the Work Backward strategy.

1. During the day long track-and-field event, Christa drank 3 more cups of water than Holly and 2 less cups of water than Kate. If Kate drank 7 cups of water, how many cups of water did each girl drink?

Think: Which girl should you start with? Why?

_____

_____

_____

2. Andy, Josh, and Molly walked from their houses to the track. Andy lives 0.75 miles from the track. Josh lives 0.28 miles further than Andy and 0.61 miles closer to the track than Molly. How far do Josh and Molly live from the track?

Think: What information will you start with?

_____

_____

_____

Name _____ Date _____

Expressions and Equations

Are the expressions 11 − (4 + 4) − 2 and (11 − 4) + (4 − 2) equal?

Simplify 11 − (4 + 4) − 2.

Step 1 Add the numbers inside the parenthesis first.

$$11 - (4 + 4) - 2$$
$$11 - 8 - 2$$

Step 2 Add or subtract from left to right.

$$11 - 8 - 2$$
$$3 - 2$$
$$1$$

Simplify (11 − 4) + (4 − 2)

Step 1 Add or subtract the numbers inside each pair of parentheses.

$$(11 - 4) + (4 - 2)$$
$$7 + 2$$

Step 2 Add or subtract from left to right.

$$7 + 2$$
$$9$$

So, $11 - (4 + 4) - 2 < (11 - 4) + (4 - 2)$.

Simplify.

1. $(6 - 2) + 11$

2. $7 - (6 - 4)$

3. $8 - (3 + 3)$

4. $9 + (4 - 1)$

_____   _____   _____   _____

5. $16 - (1.2 + 4)$

6. $(9 - 2) + 1.87$

7. $(5.22 + 2.3) - 1$

8. $(8.8 + 2) - 4.4$

_____   _____   _____   _____

9. $(2 + 8) + (7 - 4) - 6$

10. $(2.55 - 1.4) + (7 - 1)$

11. $(5.1 + 4.3) - (7 + 2.1)$

_____   _____   _____

Name _____ Date _____

Write and Evaluate Expressions

When an amount is unknown, a variable such as *x, g,* or *p*
can be used. Expressions that contain variables are called
algebraic expressions.

Write an algebraic expression.

Kim read 3 more books this summer than Casey did. We can use a variable
like *n* to stand for the number of books Casey read.

Then, *n* + 3 is the expression that shows how many books Kim read.

Evaluate the algebraic expression.

If Casey read 7 books, how many books did Kim read?

Write the expression.	Substitute 7 for *n*.	Simplify.
n + 3	7 + 3	7 + 3 = 10

If Casey read 7 books, then Kim read 10 books.

Write an algebraic expression for each word phrase.

1. Subtract a number from 27

_____

2. 4 increased by a number

_____

3. 19 plus a number

_____

4. 25 less than a number

_____

Translate each algebraic expression into words.

5. $7 + n$ **6.** $56.4 - g$ **7.** $p + 33$ **8.** $x - 28$

_____   _____   _____   _____

_____   _____   _____   _____

Evaluate each expression when *p* = 9.

9. $(23 + p) - 8$ **10.** $(p - 6) + 5$ **11.** $(3 - 2) + (p + 1)$

_____   _____   _____

Name _____   Date _____

Write and Solve Equations

Sally has a coupon for her favorite cereal. Using the coupon for
$1.00 off, Sally only had to pay $3.00 for the cereal. How much
does the cereal cost without the coupon?

Step 1 Write an equation. Use an equal sign to connect two mathematical expressions with the same value. Use the variable c to represent the regular price of cereal.	$c - 1 = 3$
Step 2 To find the correct value for c, think of the missing number.	**Think:** What number minus 1 is equal to 3?
Step 3 Write the value you found for c.	$c = 4$
Step 4 Check the result by substituting 4 for c in the original equation. The left side is equal to the right side, so $c = 4$ is correct.	$c - 1 = 3$ $4 - 1 = 3$ $3 = 3$

Solve and check.

1. $x + 3 = 5$　　　**2.** $7 + b = 10$　　　**3.** $r + 6 = 15$　　　**4.** $4 + p = 16$

5. $w + 14 = 22$　　　**6.** $8 + c = 68$　　　**7.** $q + 17 = 35$　　　**8.** $10 + n = 53$

9. $y - 5 = 13$　　　**10.** $22 - s = 9$　　　**11.** $p - 4 = 57$　　　**12.** $19 - g = 3$

13. $b - 59 = 23$　　　**14.** $77 - v = 3$　　　**15.** $x - 8 = 145$　　　**16.** $99 - e = 5$

Name _____   Date _____

Variables and Functions

A **function** is a rule that relates two variables, like *x* and *y*. For each value of *x*, there is exactly one related value of *y*.

The rule $y = 6 + x$ describes a function. What are the values of *y* when *x* is 2, 4, or 6?

To find the value of *y* for each value of *x*, substitute the value for *x* and simplify. You can organize the values in a table.

x	y
2	8
4	10
6	12

$$y = 6 + 2 \qquad y = 6 + 4 \qquad y = 6 + 6$$
$$y = 8 \qquad\quad y = 10 \qquad\quad y = 12$$

The table of values is called a **function table.**

Complete each function table.

1. $y = x + 5$

x	y
12	___
5	___
8	___
32	___

2. $y = 9 - x$

x	y
5	___
6	___
7	___
8	___

3. $y = x + 25$

x	y
5	___
4	___
3	___
2	___

4. $y = 7 - x$

x	y
2	___
___	4
1	___
___	7

5. $y = 2 + x$

x	y
3	___
5	___
7	___
9	___

6. $y = 20 - x$

x	y
8	___
9	___
___	10
___	7

7. $y = x + 8$

x	y
4	___
6	___
8	___
10	___

8. $y = x - 10$

x	y
___	5
22	___
___	18
34	___

Name _____ Date _____

Problem-Solving Application: Use an Equation

In many problems, there is some given information and an amount you need to find. You can often use an equation to help you find the unknown amount.

PROBLEM Kyle collects toy cars. He buys a red car and a yellow car for a total of $5.35. If the red car costs $3.15, how much does the yellow car cost?

Understand	What is the question?	How much does the yellow car cost?
	What do you know?	Total cost of both cars is $5.35 Cost of red car is $3.15
Plan	How can you find the answer?	Write an addition equation.
Solve	Write the equation.	cost of red car + cost of yellow car = total cost
	Substitute.	$3.15 + y = $5.35
	Solve.	$5.35 − $3.15 = y $5.35 − $3.15 = $2.20
Look Back	Estimate to check your answer. Is it reasonable?	

Use an equation to solve each money problem. Show all your work.

1. Ken can buy a comic book, which costs $2.10, or a puzzle book. If the puzzle book costs $0.75 more than the comic book, what is the cost of the puzzle book?

   Think: What will the variable in the equation represent?

   _____

2. The sale price for a jigsaw puzzle is $7.50. This is $3.25 less than it's original price. What is the original price?

   Think: Will the regular price of the jigsaw puzzle be more or less than $7.50?

   _____

3. The total cost of a cookbook and a novel is $13.98. The cookbook costs $5.35. How much does the novel cost?

4. Kathy wants to buy a CD for $21.95. She has $16.85 saved. How much more money does Kathy need to save?

   _____

Name _____ Date _____

Model the Distributive Property

Draw a rectangular array to show how you can find a product.

Step 1 Draw a rectangle that is 4 units wide and 14 units long.

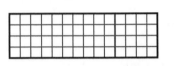

What multiplication expression describes the rectangle's area?

Would it be easier to find the area of the rectangle if you divide it into two parts?

Step 2 The diagram shows one way to divide the rectangle

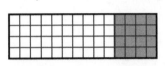

How does the rectangle show 4 × 14?

How does the rectangle show 4 × (10 + 4)?

How does the rectangle show (4 × 10) + (4 × 4)?

Step 3 Find the area of the rectangle. Use the Distributive Property.

Area = 4 × 14
= (4 × 10) + (4 × 4)
= 40 + 16
= 56

List the partial products for each and find their sums.
Then write a multiplication sentence for each.

1.

_____

2.

_____

Draw and divide a rectangle to show each product.
Use the distributive property to find the product.

3. 8 × 19

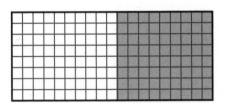

_____

4. 7 × 27

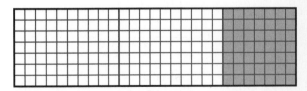

_____

Name _____ Date _____

Multiply by a One-Digit Number

Find 7 × 364.

Step 1 Multiply the ones. Regroup if you can.	$\overset{2}{3}64$ × 7 8	7 × 4 ones = 28 ones 28 ones = 2 tens + 8 ones
Step 2 Multiply the tens. Add the regrouped tens. Regroup if you can.	$\overset{42}{3}64$ × 7 48	7 × 6 tens = 42 tens 42 tens + 2 tens = 44 tens 44 tens = 4 hundred + 4 tens
Step 3 Multiply the hundreds. Add the regrouped hundreds.	$\overset{42}{3}64$ × 7 2,548	7 × 3 hundreds = 21 hundreds 21 hundreds + 4 hundreds = 25 hundreds 7 × 364 = 2,548

Find the product.
Estimate to check that your answer is reasonable.

1. 56 × 3

2. 615 × 8

3. 2,778 × 8

4. $0.84 × 8 ____

5. 4,838 × 6 ____

6. 9,314 × 3 ____

7. $3.91 × 5 ____

8. 782 × 7 ____

9. 8,113 × 6 ____

Name _____ Date _____

Multiply with Zeros

Find 4 × 509.

Step 1 Multiply the ones. Regroup if you can.	$\overset{3}{5}09$ $\times\quad 4$ ——— 6	4 × 9 = 36 ones 36 ones = 3 tens + 6 ones
Step 2 Multiply the tens. 4 × 0 tens is 0, but there are 3 regrouped tens to be added.	$\overset{3}{5}09$ $\times\quad 4$ ——— 36	4 × 0 tens = 0 tens. 0 tens + 3 tens = 3 tens.
Step 3 Multiply the hundreds.	$\overset{3}{5}09$ $\times\quad 4$ ——— 2,036	4 × 5 = 20 hundreds 509 × 4 = 2,036

Find the product. Estimate to check.

1. 204
$\times\quad 5$

2. 503
$\times\quad 2$

3. 4,002
$\times\quad 8$

4. 2,007
$\times\quad 6$

5. 4,096
$\times\quad 8$

6. 8,047
$\times\quad 5$

7. 7 × 1,405 _____

8. 82,405 × 8 _____

9. 18,505 × 3 _____

Name _____ Date _____

Problem-Solving Skill: Estimated or Exact Answers

When you solve a problem, you can sometimes use an estimate. In other situations, you need an exact answer.

Sometimes an estimate is all you need. Ryan's Scout troop hopes to raise money for new tents by selling flavored popcorn. If each of the 22 scouts raises $35, will they meet their troop's goal of $600?

The number of scouts, 22, is slightly more than 20. $20 \times \$35 = \$700$.

22 scouts will raise more than $700, so the goal will be met.

Sometimes you need an exact answer. Ryan sold 7 canisters of cheddar cheese popcorn for $4.95 each. How much money should Ryan have?

$$
\begin{array}{r}
\overset{6\ 3}{\$4.95} \\
\times\quad 7 \\
\hline
\$34.65
\end{array}
$$
       So, Ryan should have $34.65.

Answer by estimating or calculating.

1. If each new tent costs $79.95, how much would the troop have to raise in order to afford 4 new tents?

> **Think:** Should I use an estimate or calculate the exact amount to find the total cost?

_____

2. After two weeks, the troop had sold 22 tins of Cheddar Popcorn for $8 each and 9 tins of Caramel Corn for $9 each. Have they raised enough money to spend $150 at the camping supply store?

> **Think:** How can I be sure that an estimate will not be greater than the actual amount raised?

_____

Name _____ Date _____

Mental Math:
Multiply Multiples of 10, 100, and 1,000

Multiply 6 × 60,000.

Different Ways to Multiply Multiples of 10	
You can use patterns.	**You can use mental math.**
6 × 6 = 36	6 × 60,000 = 6 × 6 × 10,000
6 × 60 = 360	= 36 × 10,000
6 × 600 = 3,600	= 360,000
6 × 6,000 = 36,000	
6 × 60,000 = 360,000	

Use a pattern or mental math to find each product.

1. 4 × 40 _____   **2.** 7 × 50 _____   **3.** 8 × 90 _____

4. 3 × 80 _____   **5.** 5 × 600 _____   **6.** 7 × 200 _____

7. 400 × 30 _____   **8.** 900 × 80 _____   **9.** 60 × 700 _____

10. 20 × 800 _____   **11.** 90 × 300 _____   **12.** 500 × 30 _____

13. 80 × 4,000 _____   **14.** 20 × 9,000 _____   **15.** 70 × 6,000 _____

16. 80 × 5,000 _____   **17.** 4,000 × 90 _____   **18.** 9,000 × 10 _____

19. 30 × 7,000 _____   **20.** 20 × 5,000 _____

Name _____ Date _____

Multiplying by Multiples of 10

Multiply 54 × 30.

You can think of 54 × 30 as 54 × (3 × 10).

Step 1 Multiply 54 × 3.

$$\begin{array}{r} \overset{1}{54} \\ \times\ 3 \\ \hline 162 \end{array}$$

Step 2 Multiply the result by 10.

162 × 10 = 1,620

You can multiply multiples of 10.

Step 1 Because 30 is a multiple of 10, the ones digit in the product must be 0.

$$\begin{array}{r} 54 \\ \times\ 30 \\ \hline 0 \end{array}$$

Step 2 Multiply 54 by 3.

$$\begin{array}{r} \overset{1}{54} \\ \times\ 30 \\ \hline 1,620 \end{array}$$

Use a pattern to find each product.

1.
$$\begin{array}{r} 66 \\ \times\ 4 \\ \hline \end{array}$$

2.
$$\begin{array}{r} 66 \\ \times\ 40 \\ \hline \end{array}$$

3.
$$\begin{array}{r} 66 \\ \times\ 400 \\ \hline \end{array}$$

4.
$$\begin{array}{r} 23 \\ \times\ 5 \\ \hline \end{array}$$

5.
$$\begin{array}{r} 23 \\ \times 50 \\ \hline \end{array}$$

6.
$$\begin{array}{r} 23 \\ \times\ 500 \\ \hline \end{array}$$

7.
$$\begin{array}{r} 84 \\ \times\ 7 \\ \hline \end{array}$$

8.
$$\begin{array}{r} 84 \\ \times\ 70 \\ \hline \end{array}$$

9.
$$\begin{array}{r} 84 \\ \times\ 700 \\ \hline \end{array}$$

Name _____ Date _____

Problem-Solving Strategy: Write an Equation

Sometimes you can write an equation to solve a problem.

Iris has 5 boxes with marbles in them. She tells Lily that there
are the same number of marbles in each box, and that there are
a total of 30 marbles. How many marbles are in each box?

Understand	**What is the question?** How many marbles are in each box? **What do you know?** Iris has 5 boxes with the same number of marbles in each box and a total of 30 marbles.
Plan	**How can you find the answer?** Use an equation to find the number of marbles in each box.
Solve	**Write an equation.** Use m to represent the number of marbles in one box. $5 \times m = 30$ $m = 6$ There are 6 marbles in each box.
Look Back	**Look back at the problem.** Is your answer reasonable?

Write an equation for each problem.

1. Joaquim is thinking of a number. When
he multiplies it by 4 and subtracts 9, he
gets 31. What is Joaquim's number?

> **Think:** What is the equation for
> this problem?

_____

2. Karin's flower garden is 8 feet long and
has a perimeter of 40 feet. Find the
length of the garden.

> **Think:** How many widths and lengths
> are counted in the perimeter?

_____

3. Beth weighs 83 pounds. Beth and Steve
combined weigh twice as much as Jon.
If Jon weighs 95 pounds, how much
does Steve weigh?

> **Think:** What is the equation for
> this problem?

_____

4. Tyler's mother is 40 years old. 10 years
ago she was two times as old as Tyler is
now. How old is Tyler now?

> **Think:** What is the equation for
> this problem?

_____

Name _____   Date _____

Multiply by Two-Digit Numbers

Find 238 × 47.

Step 1 Multiply by the ones digit.	**Step 2** Multiply by the tens digit. Start by filling in a zero in the ones place.	**Step 3** Add the partial products.
25 238 × 47 — 1666	1 3 25 238 × 47 — 1666	1 3 25 238 × 47 — 1666 9520

Find each product. Estimate to check.

1.   33
× 45

2.   68
× 24

3.   81
× 31

4.   75
× 46

5.   83
× 55

6.   67
× 41

7. $0.74
×   88

8.   185
×   43

9.   803
×   72

10.   387
×   29

11. $7.98
×   43

12.   909
×   52

Name _____ Date _____

Problem-Solving Application: Use Operations

You need to decide which operation to use to solve word problems.

Sarah is signing up for horseback-riding lessons. Which is the less expensive choice if Sarah wants to take 4 hours of lessons?

Horseback-Riding Lessons
Group Lessons $18 per hour
Private Lessons $25 per hour
Buy 3, get one free!!!

Understand	**What is the question?** Which type of lesson will be less expensive if Sarah takes 4 hours of lessons? **What do you know?** Group lessons cost $18 per hour and private lessons are $25 per hour, with the 4th hour free.
Plan	**What can you do to find the answer?** Find the cost of 4 group lessons by finding $18 × 4. Find the cost of 4 private lessons by finding $25 × 3. Compare the two prices.
Solve	$18 × 4 = $72 Group lessons will cost $72.00. $25 × 3 = $75 Private lessons will cost $75.00. Private lessons will be more expensive.
Look Back	**Look back at the problem. Is your answer reasonable?** The answer is reasonable because $75 > $72.

Solve and check.

1. At the petting zoo, season passes cost $15.00 and include admission for one year and unlimited scoops of seeds for feeding the goats. Daily passes are available for $2.00 plus $0.50 per scoop of seed. Which is a better deal for someone who plans to visit the zoo 6 times this year and use 4 scoops of seed?

   Think: How can I find the total cost of visiting the petting zoo 6 times and buying 4 scoops of seed?

2. At the Horse Shop, you can rent a helmet and boots for $8 per day. At the Saddle Shop, boots cost $65 and helmets cost $39. If Omar will be at horse camp for 15 days, should he rent or buy his equipment?

   Think: How can I find the total cost of renting the equipment?

Name _____   Date _____

One-Digit Divisors

Divide. 254 ÷ 4

Step 1 Decide where to place the first digit of the quotient.	**Step 2** Divide the tens.	**Step 3** Bring down the ones. Divide the ones. Write the remainder.
Think: $4\overline{)2 \text{ hundreds}}$? hundreds	**Think:** $4\overline{)25 \text{ tens}}$? tens	**Think:** $4\overline{)14 \text{ ones}}$? ones
4 > 2 There are not enough hundreds to divide.	$\begin{array}{r} 6 \\ 4\overline{)254} \\ -24 \\ \hline 1 \end{array}$ Multiply. 6 × 4 Subtract. 25 − 24 Compare. 1 < 4	$\begin{array}{r} 63\text{ R2} \\ 4\overline{)254} \\ -24 \\ \hline 14 \\ -12 \\ \hline 2 \end{array}$ Multiply. 3 × 4 Subtract. 14 − 12 Compare. 2 < 4
$4\overline{)254}$ Place the first quotient in the tens place		

Divide.

1. $2\overline{)148}$ **2.** $6\overline{)222}$ **3.** $2\overline{)890}$ **4.** $7\overline{)231}$

5. $6\overline{)1,267}$ **6.** $5\overline{)355}$ **7.** $8\overline{)936}$ **8.** $4\overline{)210}$

9. $1,220 ÷ 5$ **10.** $168 ÷ 2$ **11.** $71,531 ÷ 8$ **12.** $322 ÷ 5$

_____   _____   _____   _____

Name _____ Date _____

Zeros in the Quotient

Divide. 1,242 ÷ 6

Step 1 Decide where to place the first digit of the quotient. Then divide.	**Step 2** Bring down the tens. Divide the tens.	**Step 3** Bring down the ones. Divide the ones.
Think: $6\overline{)1\text{ thousands}}$? thousands There are not enough thousands to divide. **Think:** $6\overline{)12\text{ hundreds}}$? hundreds $\begin{array}{r}2\\6\overline{)1242}\\-12\\\hline 0\end{array}$ Multiply. 2 × 6, Subtract. 12 − 12, Compare. 0 < 6	**Think:** $6\overline{)4\text{ tens}}$? tens There are not enough tens to divide. $\begin{array}{r}20\\6\overline{)1242}\\-12\\\hline 04\end{array}$ Write 0 in the tens place to show that the quotient has 0 tens	**Think:** $4\overline{)14\text{ ones}}$? ones $\begin{array}{r}207\\6\overline{)1242}\\-12\\\hline 042\\-42\\\hline 0\end{array}$ Multiply. 6 × 7 Subtract. 42 − 42 There is no remainder. **Check:** Multiply. 207 × 6 = 1,242

Divide.

1. $9\overline{)4,509}$ 2. $8\overline{)825}$ 3. $5\overline{)5,107}$ 4. $4\overline{)1,219}$

5. $3\overline{)625}$ 6. $9\overline{)2,078}$ 7. $3\overline{)2,109}$ 8. $7\overline{)3,507}$

9. 6,052 ÷ 6 10. 1,878 ÷ 9 11. 3,229 ÷ 4 12. 4,565 ÷ 9

Name _____ Date _____

Estimate Quotients

Estimate. 635 ÷ 8

Step 1 Decide where to place the first digit of the quotient. Then use basic multiplication facts to find a multiple of the divisor that is close to the dividend.	**Step 2** Use basic facts and multiples of 10 to estimate.

? tens **Think:** What value of n makes
8)635 $8 \times n$ close to 63?

$8 \times 8 = 64$
64 is close to 63

   80   640 is close to the dividend.
8)640

          The estimated quotient is 80.

Estimate the quotient. Tell what numbers you used for the dividend and the divisor.

1. 6)250   **2.** 5)5,790   **3.** 7)278   **4.** 4)365

_____   _____   _____   _____

_____   _____   _____   _____

5. 8)750   **6.** 5)243   **7.** 200 ÷ 7   **8.** 5,371 ÷ 6

_____   _____   _____   _____

_____   _____   _____   _____

Name _____   Date _____

Find the Mean

Find the mean of 65, 64, 61, 59, and 71.

Step 1 Add all the numbers.	**Step 2** Divide the sum by the number of addends.	**Step 3** Check your answer.
65 ⎤ 64 ⎥ 61 ⎥ — There are 59 ⎥ 5 addends. +71 ⎦ 320	$\dfrac{64}{5)\overline{320}}$	The mean, 64, is between the smallest number, 61, and the largest, 71.

Find the mean.

1. 9, 10, 15, 16, 20, 20

_____

2. 315, 385, 390, 410

_____

3. 15, 20, 20, 28, 32

_____

4. 88, 95, 102, 102, 113

_____

5. 35, 35, 35, 39

_____

6. 50, 75, 80, 92, 93

_____

7. 25, 32, 28, 35, 20

_____

8. 612, 634, 618, 625, 612, 607

_____

Problem-Solving Skill: Interpret Remainders

When you solve a problem that has a remainder, you need to decide how to interpret the remainder.

Sometimes you increase the quotient.	130 people will be attending the party. Each table seats 6 people. How many tables are needed? 130 ÷ 6 = 21 R4 22 tables are needed.
Sometimes you drop the remainder.	There are 12 cups in a pack. If 78 cups were used, how many whole packs of cups were used? 78 ÷ 12 = 6 R6 6 whole pack of cups were used.
Sometimes the remainder is the answer.	A class with 29 students went to the library in groups of 6, plus one smaller group. How many students were in the smaller group? 29 ÷ 6 = 4 R5 There were 5 students in the smaller group.

Solve.

1. John is building bookshelves. For each shelf he needs a 4 foot long piece of wood. How many bookshelves can John make from a piece of wood 19 feet long?

   Think: Can a shelf be made from a piece of wood less than 4-feet long?

2. Each shelf can hold 5 sets of books. If the library has 409 sets of books, how many shelves will be full?

   Think: Does the remainder represent a full shelf?

3. A teacher has 56 magazines to pass out. She wants to give each student 3 magazines. To how many students can she give 3 magazines?

4. Student volunteers work in the library. Each class can send only 2 volunteers. If the librarians need 27 volunteers in the library, how many classes will need to send volunteers?

Name _____   Date _____

Divide by Multiples of 10, 100, and 1,000

Basic division facts and patterns will help you divide using mental math.

Divide. 12,000 ÷ 3 = *n*

Find 12,000 ÷ 3.	
$12 \div 3 = 4$ $120 \div 3 = 40$ $1,200 \div 3 = 400$ $12,000 \div 3 = 4,000$	**Think:** What do you notice about the pattern of zeros?

Divide. Use mental math.

1. 80,000 ÷ 40   **2.** 18,000 ÷ 6   **3.** 2,400 ÷ 30

_____   _____   _____

4. 3,500 ÷ 70   **5.** 200 ÷ 20   **6.** 54,000 ÷ 900

_____   _____   _____

7. 1,800 ÷ 9   **8.** 4,200 ÷ 60   **9.** 21,000 ÷ 70

_____   _____   _____

10. 24,000 ÷ 80   **11.** 320,000 ÷ 8   **12.** 40,000 ÷ 800

_____   _____   _____

Name _____ Date _____

Divide by Two-Digit Numbers

Divide. 892 ÷ 19

Find 892 ÷ 19.

Step 1 Use an estimate to predict the first digit in the quotient. Test your prediction by dividing.

Think: 80 ÷ 20 = 4

```
    4
19)892    Multiply. 4 × 19
  −76     Subtract. 89 − 76
   13     Compare. 13 < 19
```

Step 2 Bring down the ones. Divide the ones and record the remainder.

Think: 120 ÷ 20 = 6

```
   46 R18
19)892    Multiply. 6 × 19
  −76     Subtract. 132 − 114
  132     Compare. 18 < 19
 −114
   18
```

Divide.

1. 49)350　　**2.** 24)576　　**3.** 82)869　　**4.** 68)259

5. 21)479　　**6.** 40)728　　**7.** 30)855　　**8.** 56)127

9. 23)211　　**10.** 18)539　　**11.** 15)835　　**12.** 12)529

Name _____ Date _____

Estimated Quotient Is Too Large

Divide. 458 ÷ 23

Find 458 ÷ 23.

Step 1 Estimate to place the first digit in the quotient.	**Step 2** Try a smaller number.
$\begin{array}{r} 2 \\ 23\overline{)458} \\ -46 \end{array}$ ← You can't subtract 46 from 45.	$\begin{array}{r} 19\ R21 \\ 23\overline{)458} \\ -23 \\ \hline 228 \\ -207 \\ \hline 21 \end{array}$

Divide.

1. $60\overline{)289}$

2. $31\overline{)590}$

3. $25\overline{)710}$

4. $32\overline{)459}$

5. $12\overline{)145}$

6. $55\overline{)839}$

7. $76\overline{)367}$

8. $27\overline{)734}$

9. $13\overline{)538}$

10. $34\overline{)812}$

11. $20\overline{)346}$

12. $28\overline{)460}$

13. $446 \div 94$

14. $519 \div 52$

15. $721 \div 83$

16. $368 \div 27$

_____ _____ _____ _____

Name _____   Date _____

Estimated Quotient Is Too Small

Divide. 487 ÷ 23 = *n*

Find 487 ÷ 23.

Step 1 Estimate the first digit of the quotient.	**Step 2** Try a larger number.
$$\begin{array}{r} 1 \\ 23\overline{)487} \\ -23 \\ \hline 25 \end{array}$$ ← You can make another group of 23 from this remainder. The estimated quotient is too small.	$$\begin{array}{r} 21\ R4 \\ 23\overline{)487} \\ -46 \\ \hline 27 \\ -23 \\ \hline 4 \end{array}$$

Divide.

1. $56\overline{)527}$ **2.** $45\overline{)421}$ **3.** $10\overline{)752}$ **4.** $13\overline{)489}$

5. $25\overline{)383}$ **6.** $45\overline{)467}$ **7.** $76\overline{)278}$ **8.** $12\overline{)518}$

9. $74\overline{)836}$ **10.** $33\overline{)783}$ **11.** $26\overline{)509}$ **12.** $36\overline{)735}$

Name _____   Date _____

Four- and Five-Digit Dividends

Divide. 34,876 ÷ 56   56)34,876

Find 34,876 ÷ 56.

Step 1 Estimate the first digit of the quotient. Then divide the hundreds.	**Step 2** Bring down the tens. Divide the tens.	**Step 3** Bring down the ones. Divide the ones.
Think: 60)36,000 Try 6 hundreds. $\quad\quad 6$ 56)34,876 $\underline{-33\ 6}$ $\quad\quad 1\ 2$	**Think:** 60)1,200 20 $\quad\quad 62$ 56)34,876 $\underline{-33\ 6}$ $\quad\quad 1\ 27$ $\underline{-1\ 12}$ $\quad\quad\quad 15$	**Think:** 60)120 2 $\quad\quad 622$ R44 56)34,876 $\underline{-33\ 6}$ $\quad\quad 1\ 27$ $\underline{-1\ 12}$ $\quad\quad\quad 156$ $\underline{\quad -112}$ $\quad\quad\quad\quad 44$

Divide.

1. 16)8,957

2. 39)5,682

3. 42)35,874

4. 56)2,765

5. 16)91,265

6. 8,795 ÷ 47

_____

7. 9,823 ÷ 23

8. 23,498 ÷ 30

9. 45,720 ÷ 34

_____   _____   _____

Name _____   Date _____

Problem-Solving Strategy: Draw a Diagram

Sometimes you can solve a problem by drawing a diagram.

An art museum displays paintings and sculpture. If it displays a total of 100 pieces of art, and there are 3 times as many paintings as sculptures in the museum's collection, how many paintings and how many sculptures does the museum have?

Understand	**What is the question?** How many paintings and sculptures does the museum have? **What do you know?** There are 3 times as many paintings as sculptures. There are a total of 100 pieces.
Plan	**How can you find the answer?** You can use number strips to draw a picture that represents the information.
Solve	Draw two strips. Make one strip 3 times the length of the other. Paintings ⎫ 100 Sculptures Each small rectangle must represent 25 pieces of art. There must be 25 sculptures and 75 paintings.
Look Back	Check to make sure that the total number of pieces of art in the solution matches the problem.

Draw a diagram to solve each problem.

1. The museum displays its 100 pieces of art on 3 floors. The first floor has 10 more pieces of art displayed than are displayed on the other two floors. How many pieces of art are displayed on each floor?

   Think: How many pieces of art does each rectangle represent?

   _____

   _____

2. The museum has paid workers and volunteers. There are a total of 65 workers. If there are 15 more volunteers than paid workers, how many volunteers work at the museum?

   Think: How can I find the number of volunteers?

   _____

   _____

Name _____ Date _____

Write and Evaluate Expressions

Marco works at a local grocery store. He earns $6 for every hour he works. Each paycheck, he deposits $15 in a savings account. Write an algebraic expression to show how much spending money Marco will have if he works for n hours. Then use the expression to see how much spending money he will have if he works for 20 hours.

Step 1 Write an expression for the amount Marco earns at work.	**Step 2** Subtract the amount Marco deposits in his savings account from the amount he earns at work.	**Step 3** Substitute 20 into the expression to see how much spending money Marco will have if he works for 20 hours.
If Marco works for 2 hours, he earns 2 × $6. If Marco works for n hours, he earns n × $6. You can write n × 4 in several different ways. $n \times 6 \quad 6 \times n$ $n \cdot 6 \quad 6 \cdot n$ $6n$	$(6n) - 15$ Marco earns $6n$ dollars at work and deposits 15 dollars in a savings account, so he has $(6n) - 15$ dollars in spending money when he works for n hours.	$(6n) - 15$ $= (6 \times 20) - 15$ $= 120 - 15$ $= 105$ So, if Marco works 20 hours, he will have $105 spending money.

Write each word phrase as an algebraic expression.

1. A number minus seven.

_____

2. 13 times a number

_____

3. 2 more than (4 times a number)

_____

4. 5 less than a number

_____

Write each algebraic expression in words.

5. $r - 56$

_____

6. $7x + 4$

_____

Evaluate each expression.

7. $2t - 14$ if $t = 20$

_____

8. $(4b + 2)$ if $b = 8$

_____

Name _____   Date _____

Write and Solve Equations

Solve. $p \div 8 = 5$

Different Ways to Solve an Equation

You can make a function table.

Use patterns and multiplication to complete the table.

p	$p \div 8$
64	8
56	7
48	6
40	5

$40 \div 8 = 5$, so $p = 40$

You can use inverse operations.

Multiplication and division are inverse operations.

$p \div 8 = 5$

Think: I know that a number divided by 8 is 5, so 8×5 must be equal to the number.

$40 \div 8 = 5$

$\quad p = 40$

Solve.

1. $48 = 6k$ **2.** $t \div 2 = 30$ **3.** $d - 5 = 76$ **4.** $s + 3 = 14$

_____ _____ _____ _____

5. $12 = 6m$ **6.** $45 \div p = 9$ **7.** $34 + n = 134$ **8.** $64 - h = 12$

_____ _____ _____ _____

9. $12 \times s = 60$ **10.** $4 \div r = 2$ **11.** $t + 14 = 14$ **12.** $r + 5 = 36$

_____ _____ _____ _____

Name _____   Date _____

Model Equations

If you perform the same operation on both sides of an equation, the two sides will remain equal.

The solution to $x + 7 = 13$ is $x = 6$.

Explore what happens when you do the same operation on both sides of an equation.

Add 2 to both sides.	Multiply both sides by 2.
$$\begin{array}{r} x + 7 = \ 13 \\ + 2 = +2 \\ \hline x + 9 = \ 15 \end{array}$$	$$\begin{array}{r} x + 7 = \ 13 \\ \times 2 = \times 2 \\ \hline 2(x + 7) = \ 26 \end{array} \text{ or } 2x + 14 = 26$$
The solution to the new equation is still $x = 6$.	The solution to the new equation is still $x = 6$.

Use the equation $t + 3 = 12$ for problems 1–4.

1. Solve the equation.

_____

2. Add 4 to both sides. Solve the new equation.

_____

3. Then multiply both sides by 2 and substitute the solution to the original equation in the new equation.

_____

4. Then subtract 10 from both sides. Substitute the solution to the original equation in the new equation.

_____

Name _____   Date _____

Functions and Variables

A function is a rule that gives exactly one value of y for each value of x.

Make a table for the function $y = 3 + x$

If $x = 2$, then $y = 3 + 2 = 5$

If $x = 3$, then $y = 3 + 3 = 6$

If $x = 4$, then $y = 3 + 4 = 7$

If $x = 5$, then $y = 3 + 5 = 8$

x	y
2	5
3	6
4	7
5	8

Find the value of y when $x = 6$.

1. $y = x \times 4$

2. $y = x + 2$

3. $y = (5x) + 7$

_____

_____

_____

4. $y = 7x$

5. $y = (2x) + 14$

6. $y = 3 + (5x)$

_____

_____

_____

Find the value of y when $x = 3$.

7. $y = 2 \times x$

8. $y = x + 9$

9. $y = x + 11$

_____

_____

_____

10. $y = 3x + 4$

11. $y = (3x) - 5$

12. $y = 1 + (8x)$

_____

_____

_____

Name _____ Date _____

Problem Solving Application: Use Equations

When you solve a word problem, you have to decide which operations to use.

The school had a fund-raiser carnival. There were two times as many game booths as there were craft booths. If there were 42 booths altogether, how many craft booths were there?

Understand What is the question?
How many craft booths were there?
What do you know? There were twice as many game booths as craft booths, and there were 42 booths altogether.

Plan What can you do to find the answer?
Write an equation. Let n represent the number of craft booths. $2n$ represents the number of game booths.

Solve (number of game booths) + (number of craft booths) = 42
$$2n \quad + \quad n \quad = 42$$
$$3n = 42$$
$$n = 14$$

So, there were 14 craft booths at the carnival.

Look Back Do both sides of the equation have the same value when you substitute the solution value, 14, for n?

Solve.

1. The school fund-raiser carnival took in three times as much money as the bake sale. Together they raised $500 dollars. How much money did the bake sale raise?

   Think: Do I multiply or divide to solve this problem?

   _____

2. The fund-raiser carnival was open for 4 hours. The bake sale was open half as long as the carnival was open. How many hours was the bake sale open?

   Think: Do I multiply or divide to solve this problem?

   _____

3. This year, twice the number of people came to the carnival than came last year. If 200 people came to the carnival last year, how many came this year?

   Think: Do I multiply or divide to solve this problem?

   _____

4. The dunking booth had one third the number of visitors as the ring toss. If the dunking booth had 45 visitors, how many did the ring toss have?

   Think: Do I multiply or divide to solve this problem?

   _____

Name _____   Date _____

Customary Units of Length

Measure the line segment to the nearest inch, half inch, quarter inch, and eighth inch.

To measure to the:

nearest inch	**Think:** Is the length of the line segment closer to 1 inch or 2 inches?	2 inches
nearest half inch	**Think:** Is the length of the line segment closer to $1\frac{1}{2}$ inches or 2 inches?	$1\frac{1}{2}$ inches
nearest quarter inch	**Think:** Is the length of the line segment closer to $1\frac{1}{2}$ inches or $1\frac{3}{4}$ inches?	$1\frac{1}{2}$ inches
nearest eighth inch	**Think:** Is the length of the line segment closer to $1\frac{1}{2}$ inches or $1\frac{5}{8}$ inches?	$1\frac{5}{8}$ inches

Use a ruler. Measure each line segment to the nearest inch, half inch, quarter inch, and eighth inch.

1. •————————————•   _____

2. •——————————————•   _____

3. •——————————•   _____

4. •————————————•   _____

5. •————————————————•   _____

6. •——————————————•   _____

7. •—————————•   _____

Name _____ Date _____

Perimeter and Area in Customary Units

Find the perimeter and area of each rectangle.

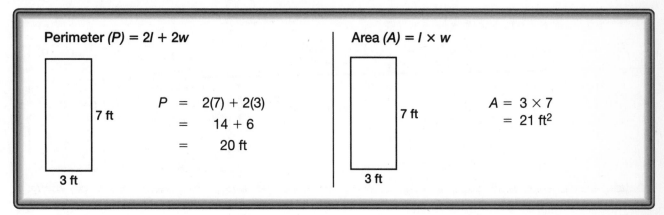

Perimeter (P) = 2l + 2w

7 ft

3 ft

$$P = 2(7) + 2(3)$$
$$= 14 + 6$$
$$= 20 \text{ ft}$$

Area (A) = l × w

7 ft

3 ft

$$A = 3 \times 7$$
$$= 21 \text{ ft}^2$$

1.

11 in.

25 in.

_____

2.

17 yd

9 yd

_____

3.

34 ft

21 ft

_____

4.

15 yd

13 yd

_____

5.

13 ft

92 ft

_____

6.

8 mi

7 mi

_____

Complete.

7. _____ in. = 3 yd

8. 14 yd = _____ ft

9. _____ in. = 11 ft

10. 2 mi = _____ ft

11. _____ in. = 5 yd

12. _____ in. = 4 ft 3 in.

13. ____ ft = 3 yd 2 ft

14. 152 in. = ___ ft ___ in.

15. 7,000 ft = ___ mi _____ ft

Name _____ Date _____

Customary Units of Weight and Capacity

Complete.

64 oz = _____ lb	Use the table to find the relationship between ounces and pounds. 16 oz = 1 lb Divide by 16 to find the number of pounds. 64 ÷ 16 = 4 64 oz = 4 lb	16 ounces (oz) = 1 pound (lb) 2,000 pounds = 1 ton (T) 8 fluid ounces (oz) = 1 cup (c) 2 cups = 1 pint (pt) 16 fluid ounces = 1 pint 2 pints = 1 quart (qt) 4 quarts = 1 gallon (gal)

1. 3 T = _____ lb

2. 18,000 lb = _____ T

3. _____ lb = 176 oz

4. 7 T = _____ lb

5. _____ oz = 8 lb

6. _____ lb = 144 oz

7. 6 qt = _____ pt

8. _____ gal = 28 qt

9. 10 c = _____ pt

10. 12 pt = _____ c

11. _____ pt = 26 qt

12. 92 oz = ____ lb ____ oz

13. 11,800 lb = _____ T _____ lb

14. 28 pt = ___ gal ___ pt

15. 23 qt = ___ gal ___ qt

Name _____ Date _____

Problem-Solving Skill: Solve Multistep Problems

Solve. Use the information from the table to help you.

School Supplies			
Notebook	$1.39	**Pencil**	$0.18
Eraser	$0.24	**Ruler**	$0.76

1. Stephanie wants to buy 2 notebooks and 3 pencils. How much money does she need?

Think: What do I need to know to find the total price?

_____

2. Which would cost more, a notebook or a ruler and 2 pencils? What is the difference in price?

Think: What is the cost of each item?

_____

3. William pays for 2 notebooks with a five-dollar bill. How much change should he get back?

Think: What do I need to find to know the amount of change?

_____

4. The store sells a package with a pencil, an eraser, and a ruler for $0.99. How much more would it cost to buy the items separately?

Think: What do I need to find to know the difference in price?

_____

5. What items could be bought for exactly $1.00?

Think: What must be true about the cost of each item?

_____

6. At the June sale, the store is selling two notebooks for $2.49. How much less do two notebooks at this price cost than two notebooks bought at the original price?

Think: What is the cost of two notebooks at the original price?

_____

Name _____ Date _____

Metric Units of Length

Use a ruler to measure this line segment to the nearest centimeter, millimeter, and decimeter.

The length is closer to 6 cm than 7 cm, so to the nearest centimeter the length is 6 cm.

To the nearest millimeter, the line segment measures 63 mm.

The length is closest to 1 dm.

centimeters

Use a ruler to measure each line segment to the nearest decimeter, centimeter, and millimeter.

1. •————————————————•

————————————————

2. •————————————————————————•

————————————————

3. •————————————————————————————•

————————————————

4. •————————————————•

————————————————

Complete.

5. 7 m = _____ cm

6. _____ dm = 6 m

7. 3,500 cm = _____ m

8. 82 dm = _____ cm

9. 8 km = _____ m

10. 19,000 m = _____ km

Name _____ Date _____

Metric Units of Mass and Capacity

Complete.

5 kg = _____ g

Metric Units of Mass
1,000 mg = 1 g
1,000 g = 1 kg
1,000 kg = 1 t

Metric Units of Capacity
1,000 mL = 1 L
1,000 L = 1 kL

Use the table to find the relationship between kilograms and grams.

1 kg = 1,000 g

Multiply by 1,000 to find the number of grams.

$5 \times 1,000 = 5,000$

5 kg = 5,000 g

1. 7 L = _____ mL

2. 9 t = _____ kg

3. 3,000 g = _____ kg

4. 15 g = _____ mg

5. 2 kg 400 g = _____ g

6. 20 L = _____ mL

7. 13,000 kg = _____ t

8. 11,000 mg = _____ g

9. 8 L 12 mL = _____ mL

Compare. Write >, <, or =.

10. 80 kg $\bigcirc$ 8,000 g

11. 5,000 mL $\bigcirc$ 7 L

12. 300 g $\bigcirc$ 3 kg

13. 12 kg $\bigcirc$ 14,000 g

14. 6,000 kg $\bigcirc$ 6 t

15. 4,000 mL $\bigcirc$ 40 L

16. 300 kg $\bigcirc$ 3 t

17. 10 L $\bigcirc$ 2,000 mL

18. 17,000 g $\bigcirc$ 17 kg

Name _____   Date _____

Add and Subtract Units of Time

How many hours and minutes are there between these times?
Find 10:44 A.M. – 3:31 P.M.

Step 1 Find the time between 10:44 A.M. and 12 noon.

$$
\begin{array}{r}
\overset{11}{\cancel{12}} \overset{60}{\cancel{00}} \text{ min} \\
-10 \text{ h } 44 \text{ min} \\
\hline
1 \text{ h } 16 \text{ min}
\end{array}
$$

Step 2 The time between 12 noon and 3:31 P.M. is 3 h 31 min.

So the total time is:

$$
\begin{array}{r}
1 \text{ h } 16 \text{ min} \\
+3 \text{ h } 31 \text{ min} \\
\hline
4 \text{ h } 47 \text{ min}
\end{array}
$$

1. 1:20 P.M. to 6:20 P.M.

_____

2. 3:16 P.M. to 5:16 P.M.

_____

3. 5:12 P.M. to 11:35 P.M.

_____

4. 12:57 A.M. to 3:22 A.M.

_____

5. 6:41 A.M. to 7:37 P.M.

_____

6. 9:37 A.M. to 1:44 P.M.

_____

7. 2:27 P.M. to 2:29 A.M.

_____

8. 10:14 A.M. to 3:56 P.M.

_____

9. 1:37 P.M. to 12:19 A.M.

_____

10. 9:12 A.M. to 4:05 P.M.

_____

Name _____ Date _____

Problem-Solving Strategy: Make a Table

Vicky recorded the height of a flower. The first week the flower was 2 inches high. The second, third, and fourth week it was 4 inches, 6 inches, and 8 inches high. When will the flower be 1 foot high?

Understand

What is the question?

When will the flower be 1 foot high?

Plan

How can you find the answer?

Make a table to calculate and record the height each day.

Week	Height
1	2
2	4
3	6
4	8
5	10
6	12

Solve

Make a table. Begin with a height of 2 inches in Week 1.

The flower will be 12 inches high in the sixth week.

Look Back Is your answer reasonable?

Solve.

1. Mandy opened a savings account. For four consecutive months, she deposited $2.00, $3.00, $4.00, and $5.00. When will she have a total of $35.00?

   Think: What pattern can you find in the increasing numbers?

   _____

2. Gerald is keeping track of how much more money he needs to buy a bicycle. For five consecutive months he needed $72.00, $64.00, $56.00, $48.00 and $40.00 more. How much longer will it take for him to have enough money to buy the bicycle?

   Think: What pattern can you find in the decreasing numbers?

   _____

3. Henry recorded the temperature every hour starting at 9:00 A.M. The first four temperatures were 63°F, 64°F, 66°F, and 69°F. If this pattern continues, when will the temperature be 78°F?

   Think: What pattern can you find in the increasing numbers?

   _____

4. It takes Sarah 5 minutes to walk 600 feet. How long will it take Sarah to walk 600 yards? 1,200 yards?

   Think: How many feet are in a yard?

   _____

Name _____ Date _____

Integers and Absolute Value

Write the absolute value of each integer.

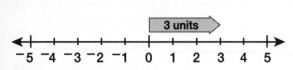

3 is 3 units from 0, so the absolute value of 3 is 3.

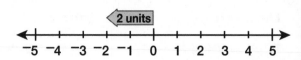

⁻2 is 2 units from 0, so the absolute value of ⁻2 is 2.

1. ⁺7   **2.** ⁻5   **3.** ⁻3   **4.** ⁻4   **5.** ⁺12

_____   _____   _____   _____   _____

6. ⁻7   **7.** ⁺17   **8.** ⁻19   **9.** ⁻12   **10.** ⁺14

_____   _____   _____   _____   _____

11. ⁺21   **12.** ⁻32   **13.** ⁻44   **14.** ⁺28   **15.** ⁺25

_____   _____   _____   _____   _____

16. ⁻38   **17.** ⁺70   **18.** ⁻52   **19.** ⁺48   **20.** ⁻92

_____   _____   _____   _____   _____

21. ⁻37   **22.** ⁻72   **23.** ⁺83   **24.** ⁻68   **25.** ⁺87

_____   _____   _____   _____   _____

26. ⁺113   **27.** ⁻108   **28.** ⁺130   **29.** ⁻122   **30.** ⁻195

_____   _____   _____   _____   _____

Name _____ Date _____

Use Models to Add Integers

Write the addition expression shown by the counters and then find the answer.

White counters represent positive numbers.

Black counters represent negative numbers.

Step 1 Combine opposites. Find all the pairs of white and black counters. Each pair of opposite counters equals zero.

Step 2 Find the sum. Leftover counters represent the sum.

There are 2 black counters remaining, so the sum is ⁻2.

$$^+5 + {}^-7 = {}^-2$$

1.

_____

2.

_____

3.

_____

4.

_____

Use two-color counters to find each sum. Record your work in your table.

5. $^+4 + {}^+4$

_____

6. $^-3 + {}^+4$

_____

7. $^-4 + {}^+1$

_____

8. $^+3 + {}^-8$

_____

9. $^-4 + {}^-3$

10. $^+2 + {}^-7$

Name _____ Date _____

Add Integers on a Number Line

Use the number line to add.

Find $^+6 + {}^-8$.

Step 1 Begin at 0. Move right 6 units to show $^+6$.

Step 2 Then move left 8 units to show $^-8$.

Step 3 The point where you stop on the number line is your answer.

$$^+6 + {}^-8 = {}^-2$$

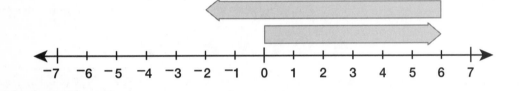

```
←|――|――|――|――|――|――|――|――|――|――|――|――|――|――→
  ⁻7  ⁻6  ⁻5  ⁻4  ⁻3  ⁻2  ⁻1   0   1   2   3   4   5   6   7
```

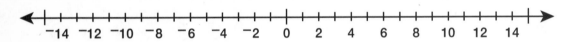

```
←|――|――|――|――|――|――|――|――|――|――|――|――|――|――|――|――→
 ⁻14 ⁻12 ⁻10  ⁻8  ⁻6  ⁻4  ⁻2   0   2   4   6   8  10  12  14
```

1. $^+5 + {}^-3$ **2.** $^-3 + {}^+2$ **3.** $^+5 + {}^-5$ **4.** $^-4 + {}^+9$

_____   _____   _____   _____

5. $^-2 + {}^-3$ **6.** $^+8 + {}^-10$ **7.** $^-10 + {}^+9$ **8.** $^-3 + {}^-6$

_____   _____   _____   _____

9. $^-11 + {}^+8$ **10.** $^-10 + {}^-3$ **11.** $^+4 + {}^-16$ **12.** $^-11 + {}^+11$

_____   _____   _____   _____

13. $^-6 + {}^+17$ **14.** $^-4 + {}^+13$ **15.** $^+12 + {}^-5$ **16.** $^+3 + {}^-8$

_____   _____   _____   _____

17. $^+9 + {}^-19$ **18.** $^-5 + {}^-9$ **19.** $^+13 + {}^-22$ **20.** $^-14 + {}^+25$

_____   _____   _____   _____

Name _____ Date _____

Use Models to Subtract

Use a model to find $^-6 - {}^+3$.

Step 1 Use black circles to represent $^-6$.  You need to take away 3 white circles, but there are none.	**Step 2** Add pairs of black and white circles as needed. This is the same as adding zero. 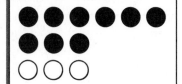	**Step 3** Subtract. The counters that are left represent the answer. 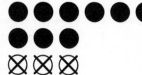 There are 9 black circles left. $^-6 - {}^+3 = {}^-9$

Use two-color counters to find each difference.

1. $^+8 - {}^+5$

_____

2. $^+4 - {}^+4$

_____

3. $^-4 - {}^-3$

_____

4. $^-3 - {}^+4$

_____

5. $^-2 - {}^+5$

_____

6. $^+4 - {}^-6$

_____

7. $^-5 - {}^-2$

_____

8. $^+4 - {}^+7$

_____

9. $^-2 - {}^-5$

_____

10. $0 - {}^+3$

_____

11. $^-1 - {}^+5$

_____

12. $^+5 - {}^-4$

_____

Name _____   Date _____

Subtract Integers on a Number Line

Find ⁻5 − ⁻3.

Step 1 Begin at 0. Move to the left 5 units to show ⁻5.

Step 2 To add ⁻3, you would move 3 units to the left. So to subtract ⁻3, move 3 units to the right.

Step 3 Your answer is where you stop on the number line.

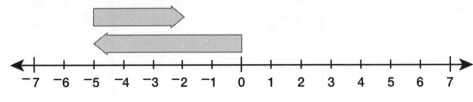

⁻5 − ⁻3 = ⁻2

Use a number line to complete each pair of number sentences.

1. ⁻2 − ⁻2 =
⁻2 + ⁺2 =

_____

2. ⁺10 − ⁺9 =
⁺10 + ⁻9 =

_____

3. ⁻1 − ⁺5 =
⁻1 + ⁻5 =

_____

4. ⁻3 − ⁻5 =
-3 + ⁺5 =

_____

5. ⁺3 − ⁺9 =
⁺3 + ⁻9 =

_____

6. ⁻4 − ⁻10 =
⁻4 + ⁺10 =

_____

Subtract. Write the related addition sentence that you used.

7. ⁻2 − ⁺3

_____

8. ⁺4 − ⁻3

_____

9. 0 − ⁻5

_____

10. ⁻1 − ⁻3

_____

11. ⁺4 − ⁺7

_____

12. ⁻10 − ⁻5

_____

Name _____   Date _____

Add and Subtract Integers

Use these rules to add and subtract integers.

1. The sum of two positive integers is positive.

2. The sum of two negative integers is negative.

3. The sum of a positive integer and a negative integer will have the same sign as the integer with the greater absolute value.

4. To subtract an integer, add its opposite. Use rules 1–3 to add.

ADDITION	SUBTRACTION
$^+4 + {}^-7 =$	$^-3 - {}^-5 =$
Since 7 has the greater absolute value, the sum will be negative.	To subtract an integer, add its opposite.
$^+4 + {}^-7 = {}^-3$	$^-3 + {}^+5 =$
	Since 5 has the greater absolute value, the sum will be positive.
	$^-3 + {}^+5 = {}^+2$

Decide if each sum or difference will be positive or negative. Then add or subtract.

1. $^-8 + {}^-3$ **2.** $^+6 + {}^-9$ **3.** $^-8 - {}^+10$ **4.** $^-8 + {}^+4$

_____   _____   _____   _____

5. $^+10 + {}^-4$ **6.** $^+5 + {}^-1$ **7.** $^-1 + {}^+3$ **8.** $^-10 - {}^-4$

_____   _____   _____   _____

9. $^-7 + {}^+5$ **10.** $^+9 + {}^-5$ **11.** $^-9 - {}^-3$ **12.** $^-9 - {}^+8$

_____   _____   _____   _____

13. $^+8 + {}^-3$ **14.** $^+4 + {}^-9$ **15.** $^+7 - {}^-4$ **16.** $^-2 - {}^+5$

_____   _____   _____   _____

Name _____ Date _____

Problem-Solving Application: Use Integers

In miniature golf, a player earns a score at each hole which is represented by an integer. At the end of the game, the sum of the scores from each hole is calculated for each player. A negative score beats a positive score. If two scores are negative, the one with the greater absolute value is better.

Mickey scored ⁻1, ⁺3, ⁻2, and ⁻1 on the first four holes. What is his score so far?

Plan	Solve
How can you find the answer? Find the sum of ⁻1, ⁺3, ⁻2, and ⁻1.	To find ⁻1 + ⁺3 + ⁻2 + ⁻1, first find ⁻1 + ⁺3 = ⁺2, then find ⁺2 + ⁻2 = 0, then find 0 + ⁻1 = ⁻1 Mickey's score so far is ⁻1

Solve.

1. On the next four holes, Mickey scored ⁻2, ⁺1, ⁺2, and 0. What is Mickey's score for these four holes?

   Think: How does 0 affect the sum of the first three integers?

   _____

2. James' score was ⁻3. On the final hole, he scored ⁻1. What was his final score? Did the last hole help or hurt his score?

   Think: Is a negative score better than a positive score?

   _____

3. Victor scored ⁻2, ⁻1, 0, and ⁺1 on the last four holes. What is his score for these four holes?

   Think: How does 0 affect the sum of the other three integers?

   _____

4. Will and Stacy played as a team. They scored ⁻3 and ⁺1. Randy and Karen played as a team and scored ⁻2 and ⁻1. Add the scores together for each team. Which team won? By how many points?

   Think: How do you find each team's total score?

   _____

Name _____   Date _____

Stem-and-Leaf Plots

The fifth grade class went to Franklin's Fruit Farm for a field trip.
The students helped pick apples and pears. The students kept
track of how many pieces of fruit they picked, and the teacher
made a stem-and-leaf plot.

Number of Apples Picked
12, 9, 25, 33, 8, 17, 14, 9, 22, 21, 13, 24, 31, 28, 21, 19

Number of Apples Picked by Each Student	
0	8, 9, 9
1	2, 3, 4, 7, 9
2	1, 1, 2, 4, 5, 8
3	1, 3

Step 1 Write a title.

Step 2 Write the tens digits needed to represent the data, in order from least to greatest. These numbers form the **stems**.

Step 3 For each piece of data, write the ones digit next to its tens digit. Arrange the **leaves** in order from least to greatest.

Number of Pears Picked by Each Student	
0	4, 6, 7
1	0, 4, 4, 4, 9
2	1, 1, 2, 5 ,6, 7
3	4, 5

Use the stem-and-leaf plot for Problems 1–5.

1. What does 3| mean?

_____

2. Which stem has six leaves? List them.

_____

3. How many students picked more than 20 pears?

_____

4. What number occurs most often? How many times does it occur?

_____

5. How many pears were picked altogether?

_____

Name _____   Date _____

Double Bar Graphs

Denny took a survey of his classmates to find out their favorite sports.

Favorite Sports

Sport	Boys	Girls
Football	9	3
Baseball	5	2
Soccer	4	13
Tennis	6	6

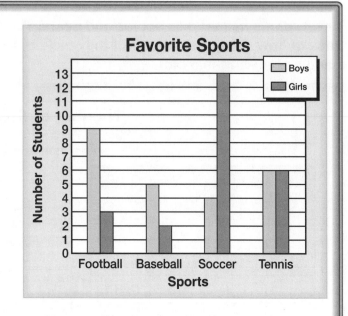

Make a double bar graph.

Step 1 Draw the axes.

Step 2 Label the vertical axis and choose a scale. Mark the intervals.

Step 3 Label the horizontal axis and list the choices.

Step 4 For each sport, draw one bar for girls and one for boys. Use different colors for boys and girls.

Step 5 Make a key to show what each color represents. Then give the graph a title.

Use the double bar graph for Problems 1–6.

1. How many more boys than girls prefer baseball?

_____

2. How many students like football?

_____

3. For what sport is there the largest difference between boys and girls?

_____

4. What is the least popular sport?

_____

5. What is the most popular sport?

_____

6. For which sport is there a difference of 6 between boys and girls?

_____

Name _____ Date _____

Histograms

Andy took a survey of the ages of people on his block and recorded the data in a frequency table. Make a histogram and use it to answer the questions.

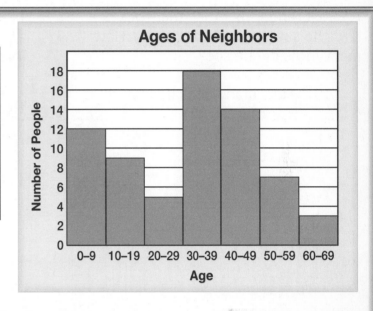

Intervals	Tally Marks	Frequency
0–9	ЖЖ ЖЖ II	12
10–19	ЖЖ IIII	9
20–29	ЖЖ	5
30–39	ЖЖ ЖЖ ЖЖ III	18
40–49	ЖЖ ЖЖ IIII	14
50–59	ЖЖ II	7
60–69	III	3

Ages of Neighbors

Step 1 Give the graph a title.

Step 2 Draw the axes. Label the horizontal axis and list the age intervals.

Step 3 Label the vertical axis. Choose a scale and mark equal intervals.

Step 4 Draw a bar for each age interval. Don't leave spaces between the bars.

Use the histogram for Problems 1–6.

1. How many more neighbors are 30–39 than 20–29?

_____

2. Which two intervals have a difference of 6?

_____

3. How many neighbors are 40 and over?

_____

4. Are more neighbors 39 and younger or 40 and older? How many more?

_____

5. Which age group has the fewest neighbors?

_____

6. How many people did Andy survey?

_____

Name _____ Date _____

Problem-Solving Skill: Choose Information From a Graph

Use information from the graphs to solve each problem.

1. A forest ranger recorded the types of birds he saw throughout the day. How many birds did he see?

Think: How many birds does each bar represent?

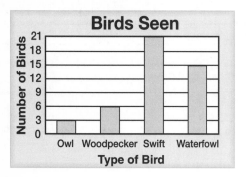

2. The circle graph shows the types of reptiles the forest ranger saw. What fraction of these reptiles are snakes?

Think: How many equal sectors are there on the circle graph?

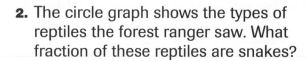
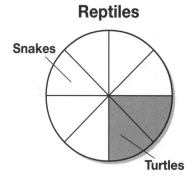

3. The graph below shows the number of visitors to the park. How many people visited the park for these four days?

Think: How many people does each bar represent?

4. The circle graph shows the types of amphibians the ranger saw one day. What fraction of amphibians were toads?

Think: How many equal sectors are there on the circle graph?

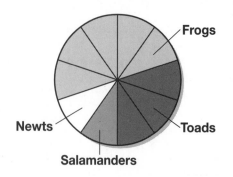

Name _____ Date _____

Mean, Median, Mode, and Range

Find the range, median, mode, and mean of 14, 23, 9, 11, 17, 11, 13.

The **range** is the difference between the greatest number and the least:

23 – 9 = 14, so the range is 14.

The **mode** is the number that occurs most often. A set of data can have more than one mode or no mode.

The mode for this data is 11.

The **median** is the middle number when the data are arranged in order.

The median number is 13.

If there are an even number of numbers, the median is the mean, or average, of the middle two numbers.

The **mean** is the sum of all the numbers divided by the number of numbers. These seven numbers have a sum of 98, so the mean is

98 ÷ 7 = 14

Find the range, median, mode, and mean for each set of data.

1. Length in centimeters
9, 20, 11, 29, 24, 15, 18

2. Time in hours
5, 7, 9, 3, 4, 8, 7, 6, 7, 8

_____

3. Age in years
12, 15, 9, 2, 13, 12, 10, 11

4. Number of students in a class
22, 29, 18, 20, 24, 29, 19, 20, 22, 20

_____

Name _____   Date _____

Line Plots

Ages of people in line for concert tickets:
13, 11, 20, 19, 14, 11, 17, 17, 16, 19, 8, 18, 16, 17, 12, 13, 17, 14, 15

What is the typical age of the people buying concert tickets?

The **range** is 20 − 8 = 12.

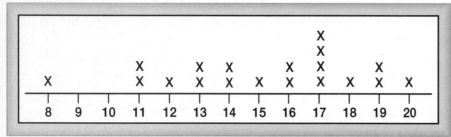

There are 19 x's, so the **median** is the 10th x, counting from left to right and bottom to top. The median is 16.	The 19 numbers have a sum of 287, so the **mean** is about 15.1. 287 ÷ 19 = 15.1052… or about 15.1

Since the mode is 17, the median is 16, and the mean is 15.1, you can say that the typical age of the people buying concert tickets is between 15 and 17.

Make a line plot for each set of data. Find the mean, median, and mode.

1. Number of coins in change
   8, 3, 5, 6, 6, 6, 8, 3, 6, 4, 2, 3

   _____

   _____

   _____

2. Daily frozen yogurt cone sales
   57, 58, 62, 55, 54, 58, 55, 51, 60, 53, 54, 55

   _____

   _____

   _____

3. Hours worked
   32, 38, 22, 38, 40, 39, 21, 19, 38

   _____

   _____

   _____

4. Inches of rain
   8, 4, 9, 12, 8, 4, 5, 9, 10, 13, 9

   _____

   _____

   _____

Name _____ Date _____

Interpret Line Graphs

Michael kept track of how far he was from his home every night on vacation. He looked at a map every night and measured the distance. When was he farthest from home?

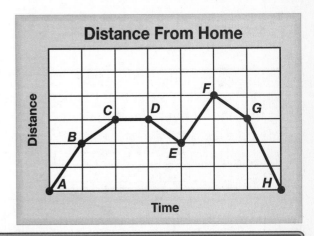

Distance From Home

Step 1 Determine what the line on the graph represents.

The line shows the distance from home. The higher the point on the graph, the farther from home Michael was.

Step 2 Determine what it means when the line rises or falls.

When the line falls, he is getting closer to home. When the line rises, he is getting farther from home.

Step 3 Find the point at which he was farthest from home.

The highest point on the graph is point *F*, so this is when he was farthest from home.

Use the line graph above to answer Problems 1–6.

1. What does point *A* represent? point *H*?

_____

_____

2. Between what two consecutive points did he travel the farthest?

_____

3. What happened between points *C* and *D*?

_____

_____

4. What happened between points *D* and *E*?

_____

Use the graph at the right for problems 5 and 6.

5. What happened between points *C* and *D*?

_____

6. Between what points did the most driving occur?

_____

_____

Distance Driven

Name _____   Date _____

Line and Double Line Graphs

Mr. Wilkins keeps track of his bank balances.
At the end of every month, he records his balances.

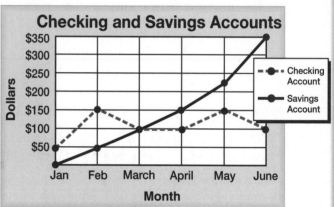

What was the first month Mr. Wilkins had more than $100 in his
Christmas account?

Look at the Christmas account line graph. The first point that is
above $100 is in May, so this is the first month he had more
than $100 in the account.

Use the graphs for Problems 1–6.

1. What does the graph tell you about
the amount of money in Mr. Wilkins'
Christmas account from January
to June?

_____

2. How much money was deposited into
the savings account during May?

_____

3. How many ordered pairs of data are
shown in the line graph?

_____

4. During what month did Mr. Wilkins
deposit the most money into the
Christmas account? How much?

_____

5. When did Mr. Wilkins' checking and
savings account have the same balance?
What was the balance?

_____

6. What was the total of Mr. Wilkins'
checking and savings accounts
at the end of May?

_____

Name _____ Date _____

Choose an Appropriate Graph

Which type of graph would you use to show the information given in the table?

Number of movie screens in Taylor County	
1980	25
1985	35
1990	50
1995	15
2000	20

Different Ways to Graph Data

A **bar graph** is a good choice when the data can be counted and you want to make comparisons.

A **line graph** is appropriate when you want to show changes over time.

A **pictograph** is a good choice when the data are multiples of a number.

A **circle graph** is a good choice when the data are parts of a whole.

A **histogram** is a good choice to show how often something happens within equal intervals.

Since all the numbers are multiples of 5, you could use a pictograph.
Since the data shows change over time, you could use a line graph.

Choose an appropriate graph for the data given.

1.

Class Pets at Hillmore Elementary	
Pet	**Number**
Fish	16
Hamsters	4
Snakes	2
Gerbils	5
Turtles	8

2.

Class Pets in Mrs. Bear's Room	
Pet	**Number**
Fish	3
Hamsters	1
Gerbils	2
Turtles	2
Total:	8

3.

Pet Ages at Hillmore Elementary	
Age	**Number**
0–2 years	4
2–4 years	9
4–6 years	8
6–8 years	7
8–10 years	2

4.

Length of Sammy the Snake	
Age	**Length**
1 month	4 inches
2 months	8 inches
3 months	12 inches
4 months	15 inches
5 months	17 inches

Name _____   Date _____

Problem-Solving Strategy: Make a Table

Tyler found the following information for his report on U.S. Currency. The table lists the people whose images are on each kind of coin and paper currency. Use the table to solve each problem.

People Appearing on Selected U.S. Currency

Paper Currency		Coins	
Denomination	Person	Denomination	Person
$1	George Washington	Penny	Abraham Lincoln
$2	Thomas Jefferson	Nickel	Thomas Jefferson
$5	Abraham Lincoln	Dime	Franklin Delano Roosevelt
$10	Alexander Hamilton	Quarter	George Washington
$20	Andrew Jackson	Half-dollar	John F. Kennedy
$50	Ulysses S. Grant	$1	Susan B. Anthony
$100	Benjamin Franklin	Golden $1	Sacagawea and infant son

How many people appear on both a coin and a paper denomination?

Plan Check off each name that occurs in both tables.

Solve George Washington, Thomas Jefferson and Abraham Lincoln appear in both tables.

So, 3 people appear on both a coin and paper denomination.

1. How many people who appear on a paper denomination do not appear on a coin?

   Think: What information will I start with?

   _____

2. Who appears on paper currency worth 4 times the amount of the coin on which they appear?

   Think: How can I organize the information?

   _____

3. Who appears on paper currency worth 500 times the amount of the coin on which they appear?

   Think: How can I organize the information?

   _____

4. Who appears on paper currency worth 40 times the amount of the coin on which they appear?

   Think: How can I organize the information?

   _____

Name _____ Date _____

Make Choices

Bradley can choose either a sandwich or soup and salad for lunch. He can choose either an apple, a pear, or a banana for desert. How many different choices does he have for lunch?

Different Ways to Make Choices

You can make an organized list.

sandwich, apple
sandwich, pear
sandwich, banana
soup and salad, apple
soup and salad, pear
soup and salad, banana

You can make a tree diagram.

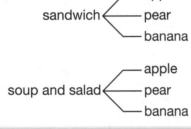

You can also multiply to find all the possible outcomes.

Look at the tree diagram.

meal × desert = number of
choices   choices   outcomes

2   ×   3   =   6

Bradley can combine lunches and deserts in 6 different ways.
Make an organized list to show all possible choices.

1.

Vacation Choices	
Travel by	**Destination**
airplane	California
car	Florida
bus	

_____
_____
_____
_____

2.

Pizza Choices	
Crust	**Toppings**
thin	cheese
thick	onion
	green peppers
	mushrooms

_____
_____
_____
_____

Multiply to find the number of choices possible if you can make one choice from each category.

3. 4 meals, 5 deserts

4. 3 paper sizes, 8 paper colors

5. 4 pants, 7 shirts

_____   _____   _____

Name _____ Date _____

Probability

The spinner shown is used for a game. If the spinner lands on black, player A wins. If the spinner lands on white, player B wins. If the spinner lands on the striped section, player C wins. Is this game fair?

When a player spins, there are three possible outcomes. The spinner can land on black, white, or striped. Since the black section is largest, the spinner is more likely to land on black than on the white or striped sections.

Solution: Player A will win most often, so the game is not fair.

The probability of an event is the likelihood of the event occurring. You can show probability on a number line from 0 to 1, where 0 describes an impossible event, and 1 describes an event that is certain to occur.

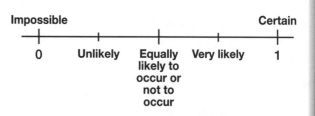

Use the spinner for Problems 1–7. Tell whether each event is *equally likely*, *very likely*, *unlikely*, *certain*, or *impossible*.

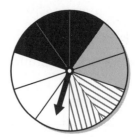

1. black

_____

2. striped

_____

3. grey

_____

4. striped or grey

_____

5. white or black

_____

6. striped, grey, black, or white

_____

7. dotted

_____

8. grey, black, or white

_____

Name _____ Date _____

Find Probability

If you pick a shape from the bag, what is the probability that it will be a circle?

Find the probability of picking a circle.

$$\frac{\text{number of circles}}{\text{total number of shapes}} = \frac{5}{15} = \frac{1}{3}$$

The probability of picking a circle is $\frac{1}{3}$.

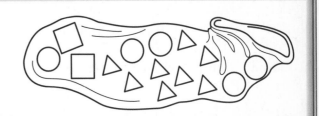

Use the shapes to answer the problems. If the shapes are placed in the bag, picked without looking, and then put back, what is the probability of each event.

1. a black circle

2. a dotted circle

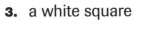

3. a white square

4. a white circle

5. a white shape

6. a black or dotted square

7. a black circle or a dotted square

8. a white or dotted shape

Name _____ Date _____

Problem-Solving Application: Use Data

A gas grill uses a tank of propane. The chart shows how long a gas grill can be fueled by 1 tank of propane. 60 grills were tested. What is the probability that a grill will be fueled for longer than 120 minutes on a tank of propane?

Propane Tank Times		
Time (minutes)	Tally	Frequency
0–30		8
31–60		12
61–90		3
91–120		11
121–150		22
151–180		4

Understand

What is the question? What is the probability that a grill will be fueled longer than 120 minutes?

What do you know? 60 grills were tested. The chart shows how long each grill was fueled by one tank of propane.

Plan

How can you find the answer?
Use the formula for probability:

$P = \dfrac{\text{number of favorable outcomes}}{}$

Solve

Use the number of grills which were fueled for longer than 120 minutes as the favorable outcomes.
Use the number of grills tested as the number of possible outcomes.

$P = \dfrac{22 + 4}{60} = \dfrac{26}{60} = \dfrac{13}{30}$

Use the chart to solve each problem.

1. What fraction of the grills tested were fueled for one hour or less?

_____

2. What is the probability that a grill will run 90 minutes or less on a tank of propane?

_____

3. What is the probability that a grill can be used for 3 hours or less?

_____

4. What is the probability that a grill can be used for more than 4 hours?

_____

Name _____ Date _____

Prime and Composite Numbers

A **prime number** is a counting number greater than 1 whose only factors are 1 and the number.

A **composite number** is a counting number that has more than two factors.

Is 13 a prime number?

Check all the counting numbers from 1 to 13.

The only factors are 1 and 13.

$$1 \times 13 = 13$$

The number 13 is a prime number.

Is 30 a prime or composite number?

Check all counting numbers from 1 to 30.

The factors of 30 are 1, 2, 3, 5, 6, 10, 15, 30.

$$1 \times 30 = 30 \qquad 2 \times 15 = 30$$
$$3 \times 10 = 30 \qquad 5 \times 6 = 30$$

The number 30 is a composite number because it has more than two factors.

Identify each number as *prime* or *composite*. Write each composite number as a product of two factors that are either prime or composite numbers.

1. 7

_____

_____

2. 40

_____

_____

3. 10

_____

_____

4. 4

_____

_____

5. 19

_____

_____

6. 49

_____

_____

7. 35

_____

_____

8. 39

_____

_____

Name _____   Date _____

Prime Factorization

Find the prime factorization of 60.

Step 1 Write 60 as the product of two factors. Do not use 1 as a factor.	**Step 2** Write each factor as a product of two factors until all factors are prime numbers.	**Step 3** Write all the factors in order. Then, use exponents to write the prime factorization.
60 2 × 30	60 2 × 30 2 × 6 × 5 2 × 2 × 3 × 5	$60 = 2 \times 2 \times 3 \times 5$ $= 2^2 \times 3 \times 5$

What factor completes each factor tree?

1.   15
3 × ■

_____

2.   21
■ × 3

_____

3.   9
3 × ■

_____

4.   18
9 × 2
3 × 3 × ■

_____

5.   54
9 × 6
3 × ■ × 2 × 3

_____

6.   32
4 × 8
2 × 2 × 4 × 2
2 × 2 × ■ × 2 × 2

_____

7.   90
9 × 10
3 × 3 × ■ × 2

_____

8.   44
11 × 4
11 × ■ × 2

_____

9.   20
5 × 4
5 × 2 × ■

_____

Name _____ Date _____

Divisibility

Test whether each number below is divisible by 2, 3, 4, 5, 9, and 10.

124, 380, 816, 435, 990, 315

	124	380	816	435	990	315
Step 1 Check for divisibility by 2. The number must end with 0, 2, 4, 6, or 8. **Example:** 124 ends in 4, so it is divisible by 2.	x	x	x		x	
Step 2 Check for divisibility by 5. The number must end with 0 or 5. **Example:** 124 ends in 4, so it is not divisible by 5.		x		x	x	x
Step 3 Check for divisibility by 10. **Example:** 380 ends in 0, so it is divisible by 10.		x			x	
Step 4 Check for divisibility by 4. The last 2 digits must be divisible by 4. **Example:** 124 ends with 24, so it is divisible by 4.	x	x	x			
Step 5 Check for divisibility by 3. The sum of the digits must be divisible by 3. **Example:** 990: 9 + 9 + 0 = 18, which is divisible by 3, so 990 is divisible by 3.			x	x	x	x
Step 6 Check for divisibility by 9. The sum of the digits must be divisible by 9. **Example:** 990: 9 + 9 + 0 = 18, which is divisible by 9, so 990 is divisible by 9.					x	x

990 is divisible by 2, 3, 5, 9 and 10.

Test each number to see if it is divisible by 2, 3, 4, 5, 9, or 10.

	Number	Divisible by
1.	325	
2.	678	
3.	180	
4.	142	

	Number	Divisible by
5.	648	
6.	1,124	
7.	1,890	
8.	3,091	

Name _____ Date _____

Common Factors and Greatest Common Factor

Find the common factors and the greatest common factor
of 40 and 45.

Step 1 List all the factors of each number.
40: 1, 2, 4, 5, 8, 10, 20, 40
45: 1, 3, 5, 9, 15, 45

Step 2 Find the factors that are in both lists.
The common factors of 40 and 45 are 1 and 5.

Step 3 Compare the common factors to find the greatest common factor (GCF).
The greatest common factor of 40 and 45 is 5.

**List the factors for each number. Find the greatest common factor
(GCF) for each pair of numbers.**

1. 4, 10   **2.** 12, 14   **3.** 6, 21   **4.** 7, 9   **5.** 13, 26

_____   _____   _____   _____   _____

_____   _____   _____   _____   _____

_____   _____   _____   _____   _____

6. 40,48   **7.** 20, 30   **8.** 12, 18   **9.** 4, 80   **10.** 25, 50

_____   _____   _____   _____   _____

_____   _____   _____   _____   _____

_____   _____   _____   _____   _____

11. 40, 50   **12.** 15, 35   **13.** 16, 20   **14.** 3, 26   **15.** 8, 16

_____   _____   _____   _____   _____

_____   _____   _____   _____   _____

_____   _____   _____   _____   _____

Name _____ Date _____

Common Multiples and Least Common Multiple

Find the least common multiple of 9 and 12.

Step 1 List the multiples of both numbers. 9: 9, 18, 27, **36**, 45, 54, 63, **72**,.... 12: 12, 24, **36**, 48, 60, **72**, 84,...	**Step 2** List the common multiples. 36, 72, ...	**Step 3** Find the Least Common Multiple (LCM). The LCM is 36.

Find the LCM of 9 and 12 by using the prime factorization.

Step 1 Use factor trees to find the prime factorizations, of the two numbers. 9 3 × 3 12 6 × 2 3 × 2 × 2	**Step 2** List all the prime factors of the two numbers including repeated primes. 9: 3, 3 12: 2, 2, 3	**Step 3** Determine the LCM. Multiply all the factors, using the common factors only once. The common factor, 3, is used once. The LCM of 9 and 12 is 2 × 2 × 3 × 3 or 36.

List multiples to find the LCM. Then use the prime factorization method.

1. 10, 15   **2.** 8, 10   **3.** 15, 30   **4.** 12, 21

_____   _____   _____   _____

5. 8, 10   **6.** 9, 15   **7.** 7, 21   **8.** 5, 9

_____   _____   _____   _____

9. 2, 7   **10.** 4, 12   **11.** 1, 3   **12.** 14, 21

_____   _____   _____   _____

Name _____ Date _____

Problem-Solving Strategy: Use Logical Thinking

Problem: What two numbers have an LCM of 180, a GCF of 6, and a sum of 78?

Understand	Question: What are the 2 unknown numbers? Given: They have an LCM of 180, GCF of 6, and a sum of 78.
Plan	Solve using logical reasoning.
Solve	**Start by factoring the LCM.** $180 = 2 \times 2 \times 3 \times 3 \times 5$. If 6 is the GCF, then the remaining 2, 3, and 5 cannot be common factors.

Make Venn diagrams to try different arrangements.
The 6 should be inside both circles because it is a factor of both numbers.
Each of the other factors should be inside one circle but not both.

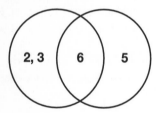

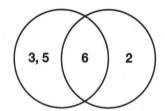

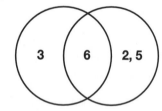

$$2 \times 3 \times 6 = 36$$
$$5 \times 6 = 30$$

$$3 \times 5 \times 6 = 90$$
$$2 \times 6 = 12$$

$$3 \times 6 = 18$$
$$2 \times 5 \times 6 = 60$$

Look for a pair of numbers with a sum of 78. The numbers are 60 and 18.

Solve these problems using the Logical Thinking strategy.

1. The LCM of two numbers is 120. The GCF is 4. They differ by 4. What are the two numbers?

    What do you know about the LCM?

2. The GCF of two different numbers is 16. Both of these numbers are greater than 48 but less than 96. What are the numbers?

    What do you know about the prime factors of the number?

Name _____   Date _____

Write Fractions

A unit fraction is a fraction with a numerator of 1. You can represent fractions on a number line. If intervals of length 1 on the number line are divided into 5 equal pieces, the length of any one of the pieces represents $\frac{1}{5}$.

The unit fraction $\frac{1}{5}$ can also be thought of as $1 \div 5$ since the unit interval is divided into 5 equal parts.

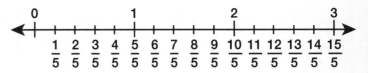

Write each missing fraction. Then draw a picture to represent each missing fraction.

1.

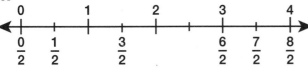

_____

2.

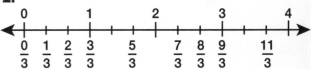

_____

3.

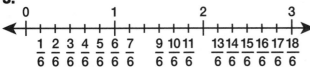

_____

4.

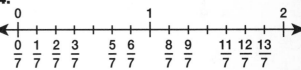

_____

5.

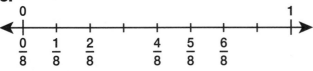

_____

6.

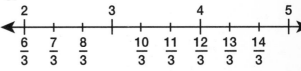

_____

Name _____ Date _____

Equivalent Fractions

Two fractions that name the same amount are called equivalent fractions.

Find a fraction equivalent to $\frac{2}{3}$.

One Way: Using a Number Line

The number lines show thirds and sixths.

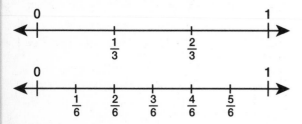

The fractions $\frac{2}{3}$ and $\frac{4}{6}$ are at the same position on the number lines.

So, $\frac{2}{3} = \frac{4}{6}$.

Another Way: Equivalent Fraction Rule

The rule states that if the numerator and denominator of a fraction are each multiplied by the same counting number, then the new fraction represents the same number.

$$\frac{2}{3} = \frac{2 \times 2}{3 \times 2} = \frac{4}{6} \qquad \frac{2}{3} = \frac{2 \times 3}{3 \times 3} = \frac{6}{9} \qquad \frac{2}{3} = \frac{2 \times 4}{3 \times 4} = \frac{8}{12}$$

So, $\frac{2}{3}$, $\frac{4}{6}$, $\frac{6}{9}$, and $\frac{8}{12}$ are equivalent fractions.

For each fraction, write two equivalent fractions.

1. $\frac{1}{2}$

_____

2. $\frac{1}{6}$

_____

3. $\frac{4}{7}$

_____

4. $\frac{2}{9}$

_____

5. $\frac{5}{12}$

_____

6. $\frac{4}{9}$

_____

7. $\frac{5}{10}$

_____

8. $\frac{9}{12}$

_____

9. $\frac{1}{8}$

_____

10. $\frac{5}{6}$

_____

11. $\frac{8}{9}$

_____

12. $\frac{2}{5}$

_____

13. $\frac{2}{7}$

_____

14. $\frac{3}{10}$

_____

15. $\frac{7}{16}$

_____

16. $\frac{9}{20}$

_____

Name _____ Date _____

Simplest Form

Find the simplest form of the fraction $\frac{8}{20}$.

Step 1 Find the greatest common factor (GCF) of the numerator and denominator.

$$8 = 2 \times 2 \times 2$$
$$20 = 2 \times 2 \times 5$$

The GCF of 8 and 20 is $2 \times 2 = 4$.

Step 2 Use the GCF to write an equivalent fraction.

$$\frac{8}{20} = \frac{8 \div 4}{20 \div 4} = \frac{2}{5}$$

The simplest form of $\frac{8}{20}$ is $\frac{2}{5}$.

Simplify each fraction.

1. $\frac{4}{10}$ _____ 2. $\frac{6}{9}$ _____ 3. $\frac{5}{15}$ _____ 4. $\frac{2}{5}$ _____ 5. $\frac{9}{27}$ _____

6. $\frac{10}{100}$ _____ 7. $\frac{7}{9}$ _____ 8. $\frac{30}{40}$ _____ 9. $\frac{8}{18}$ _____ 10. $\frac{6}{30}$ _____

11. $\frac{12}{81}$ _____ 12. $\frac{6}{24}$ _____ 13. $\frac{13}{20}$ _____ 14. $\frac{14}{21}$ _____ 15. $\frac{2}{18}$ _____

16. $\frac{8}{24}$ _____ 17. $\frac{6}{12}$ _____ 18. $\frac{14}{52}$ _____ 19. $\frac{9}{27}$ _____ 20. $\frac{2}{9}$ _____

Name _____ Date _____

Fractions, Decimals, and Mixed Numbers

Compare: 0.4 ◯ $\frac{4}{5}$

Different Ways to Write Numbers	
You can write the decimal as a fraction.	You can write a fraction as a decimal.
$0.4 = \frac{4}{10} = \frac{2 \times 2}{2 \times 5} = \frac{2}{5}$	$\frac{4}{5} = \frac{4 \times 2}{5 \times 2} = \frac{8}{10} = 0.8$
$\frac{2}{5} < \frac{4}{5}$, so $0.4 < \frac{4}{5}$	$0.4 < 0.8$, so $0.4 < \frac{4}{5}$

Change $\frac{11}{5}$ to a mixed number.

$\frac{11}{5} = \frac{5}{5} + \frac{5}{5} + \frac{1}{5} = 1 + 1 + \frac{1}{5} = 2\frac{1}{5}$

Write each as a fraction or mixed number.

1. 0.9 _____   **2.** 5.6 _____   **3.** $\frac{15}{4}$ _____   **4.** $\frac{45}{7}$ _____

Write each fraction as a decimal.

5. $\frac{6}{10}$ _____   **6.** $\frac{9}{2}$ _____   **7.** $4\frac{1}{4}$ _____   **8.** $\frac{5}{1}$ _____

Compare. Write <, >, or = for each ◯.

9. $\frac{1}{3}$ ◯ $\frac{5}{6}$ **10.** $\frac{1}{10}$ ◯ 0.5   **11.** $4\frac{1}{4}$ ◯ 4.6   **12.** $\frac{1}{5}$ ◯ 0.2

13. $2\frac{1}{2}$ ◯ 2.7   **14.** 0.7 ◯ $\frac{13}{20}$ **15.** 4.25 ◯ $\frac{17}{4}$ **16.** 1.85 ◯ $1\frac{7}{10}$

Name _____ Date _____

Compare Fractions

Two fractions that have the same denominator are said to have a **common denominator**. In order to compare fractions, they must have a common denominator.

Compare $\frac{2}{5}$ and $\frac{1}{3}$.
Find equivalent fractions with a common denominator.

Step 1 Multiply the numerator and denominator of the first fraction by the denominator of the second fraction.	**Step 2** Multiply the numerator and denominator of the second fraction by the denominator of the first fraction.	**Step 3** Compare the fractions.
$\frac{2}{5} = \frac{2 \times 3}{} = \frac{6}{15}$	$\frac{1}{3} = \frac{1 \times 5}{3 \times 5} = \frac{5}{15}$	$6 > 5$ So $\frac{6}{15} > \frac{5}{15}$ $\frac{2}{5} > \frac{1}{3}$

Compare these numbers. Write >, <, or = for each $\bigcirc$.

1. $\frac{5}{6} \bigcirc \frac{3}{5}$

2. $1\frac{9}{11} \bigcirc 1\frac{5}{6}$

3. $3\frac{2}{7} \bigcirc 3\frac{1}{9}$

4. $\frac{3}{5} \bigcirc \frac{5}{8}$

5. $\frac{2}{3} \bigcirc \frac{5}{6}$

6. $1\frac{3}{5} \bigcirc 1\frac{3}{8}$

7. $\frac{5}{12} \bigcirc \frac{1}{5}$

8. $\frac{7}{9} \bigcirc \frac{3}{4}$

9. $\frac{4}{15} \bigcirc \frac{3}{10}$

10. $2\frac{2}{3} \bigcirc 2\frac{1}{2}$

11. $1\frac{4}{5} \bigcirc 2\frac{2}{5}$

12. $4\frac{5}{6} \bigcirc 4\frac{7}{8}$

Name _____ Date _____

Problem Solving Skill: Is the Answer Reasonable?

It is important to look back at the original question to see if your answer is reasonable. Answers or statements may be unreasonable if the problem has been misinterpreted, the answer does not make sense, or the calculations are incorrect.

> Jan is 14. Mark is twice her age and Kirk is half her age.
>
> The student wrote on the test "Mark is 7 and Kirk is 28."
>
> The student misinterpreted the problem and therefore the answer is unreasonable. Mark is twice Jan's age ($14 \times 2 = 28$). Kirk is half her age ($14 \div 2 = 7$).

Tell whether each statement is reasonable or unreasonable. Explain your answer.

1. On Monday at Lincoln Elementary $\frac{1}{2}$ of the children brought lunch from home. The other children bought lunch in the cafeteria. About $\frac{2}{3}$ of the children got lunch in the cafeteria on Monday.

   Think: How many children brought their lunch?

   _____

   _____

   _____

2. 12 people had a hot dog at the party and 15 people had a hamburger. $\frac{12}{15}$ of the people had a hot dog.

   Think: How many people total ate a hot dog and hamburger?

   _____

   _____

   _____

3. Dan canoed 9 miles each day for a week. He canoed 63 miles.

   Think: How many days are in a week?

   _____

   _____

4. Kent had $15.23 and spent $ 5.15 on food. The cashier gave him $ 7.01 in change.

   Think: Estimate how much should be left.

   _____

   _____

   _____

Name _____ Date _____

Add and Subtract Fractions With Like Denominators

Fractions that have the same denominator are called like fractions.

Find $\frac{5}{6} + \frac{3}{6}$.	Find $\frac{10}{12} - \frac{7}{12}$.
To add like fractions, add the numerators and keep the same denominator.	To subtract like fractions, subtract the numerators and keep the same denominator.
$\frac{4}{6} + \frac{3}{6} = \frac{7}{6}$	$\frac{10}{12} - \frac{7}{12} = \frac{3}{12}$
The sum is greater than one so change to a mixed number.	The difference can be simplified.
$\frac{7}{6} = 1\frac{1}{6}$	$\frac{3}{12} = \frac{3 \div 3}{12} = \frac{1}{4}$

Add or subtract. Show each answer in simplest form.

1. $\frac{1}{8} + \frac{4}{8}$ **2.** $\frac{1}{4} + \frac{3}{4}$ **3.** $\frac{8}{15} - \frac{2}{15}$ **4.** $\frac{3}{6} + \frac{1}{6}$ **5.** $\frac{3}{4} - \frac{1}{4}$

_____   _____   _____   _____   _____

6. $\frac{4}{5} + \frac{4}{5}$ **7.** $\frac{4}{5} - \frac{1}{5}$ **8.** $\frac{9}{10} - \frac{1}{10}$ **9.** $\frac{3}{7} + \frac{2}{7}$ **10.** $\frac{1}{9} + \frac{2}{9}$

_____   _____   _____   _____   _____

11. $\frac{5}{9} - \frac{3}{9}$ **12.** $\frac{8}{9} + \frac{5}{9}$ **13.** $\frac{1}{2} + \frac{3}{2}$ **14.** $\frac{11}{24} - \frac{1}{24}$ **15.** $\frac{1}{6} + \frac{1}{6}$

_____   _____   _____   _____   _____

16. $\frac{5}{7} + \frac{4}{7}$ **17.** $\frac{9}{15} - \frac{4}{15}$ **18.** $\frac{1}{5} + \frac{3}{5}$ **19.** $\frac{7}{12} - \frac{1}{12}$ **20.** $\frac{1}{3} + \frac{2}{3}$

_____   _____   _____   _____   _____

Name _____   Date _____

Add Fractions With Unlike Denominators

Add $\frac{1}{6} + \frac{1}{4} = n$.

You cannot add the unit fraction $\frac{1}{6}$ and the unit fraction $\frac{1}{4}$ because they are different units. You need to find equivalent fractions with a common denominator.

Step 1 Multiply numerator and denominator of the first fraction by the denominator of the second.	**Step 2** Multiply numerator and denominator of the second fraction by the denominator of the first.	**Step 3** Add the equivalent fractions and simplify if possible.
$\frac{1}{6} = \frac{1 \times 4}{} = \frac{4}{24}$	$\frac{1}{4} = \frac{1 \times 6}{} = \frac{6}{24}$	$\frac{1}{6} + \frac{1}{4} = \frac{4}{24} + \frac{6}{24} = \frac{10}{24}$ $\frac{10}{24} = \frac{2 \times 5}{} = \frac{5}{12}$

Add. Write each sum in simplest form.

1. $\frac{1}{10}$
$+ \frac{2}{12}$

2. $\frac{2}{5}$
$+ \frac{1}{10}$

3. $\frac{2}{4}$
$+ \frac{3}{6}$

4. $\frac{9}{10}$
$+ \frac{1}{5}$

5. $\frac{5}{8}$
$+ \frac{2}{3}$

6. $\frac{1}{3}$
$+ \frac{2}{9}$

7. $\frac{7}{8}$
$+ \frac{2}{5}$

8. $\frac{3}{8}$
$+ \frac{1}{4}$

9. $\frac{5}{11}$
$+ \frac{1}{2}$

10. $\frac{3}{7}$
$+ \frac{1}{5}$

11. $\frac{1}{2} + \frac{1}{6}$ _____

12. $\frac{1}{4} + \frac{3}{5}$ _____

13. $\frac{3}{5} + \frac{1}{15}$ _____

14. $\frac{5}{6} + \frac{4}{7}$ _____

15. $\frac{2}{7} + \frac{1}{5}$ _____

16. $\frac{1}{6} + \frac{1}{12}$ _____

17. $\frac{9}{11} + \frac{3}{22}$ _____

18. $\frac{8}{100} + \frac{2}{10}$ _____

Name _____   Date _____

Use the LCD to Add Fractions

Find $\frac{1}{6} + \frac{3}{8}$.

Step 1 Find the least common multiple (LCM) of the denominators. This is the least common denominator (LCD).

$6 = 2 \times 3$
$8 = 2 \times 2 \times 2$
The LCM is $2 \times 2 \times 2 \times 3 = 24$

Step 2 Use the LCM as a common denominator to find equivalent fractions.

$\frac{1}{6} = \frac{1 \times 4}{6 \times 4} = \frac{4}{24}$
$\frac{3}{8} = \frac{3 \times 3}{8 \times 3} = \frac{9}{24}$

Step 3 Add the equivalent fractions and simplify if possible.

$\frac{4}{24} + \frac{9}{24} = \frac{13}{24}$

Add. Write each sum in simplest form.

1. $\frac{2}{9} + \frac{1}{3}$

2. $\frac{1}{8} + \frac{3}{6}$

3. $\frac{3}{4} + \frac{1}{2}$

4. $\frac{9}{10} + \frac{1}{5}$

5. $\frac{5}{8} + \frac{2}{3}$

6. $\frac{1}{10} + \frac{3}{20}$

7. $\frac{3}{8} + \frac{1}{2}$

8. $\frac{2}{9} + \frac{4}{5}$

9. $\frac{1}{4} + \frac{2}{3}$

10. $\frac{1}{6} + \frac{1}{3}$

11. $\frac{4}{5} + \frac{3}{15}$

12. $\frac{1}{8} + \frac{1}{6}$

13. $\frac{3}{4} + \frac{1}{6}$

14. $\frac{5}{7} + \frac{4}{5}$

15. $\frac{9}{10} + \frac{1}{2}$

16. $\frac{1}{2} + \frac{1}{6}$

Name _____   Date _____

Add Mixed Numbers

In order to add fractions, you need to have a common denominator.

Add. $2\frac{3}{10} + 3\frac{1}{10} = n$

Step 1 Add the fractions.	**Step 2** Add the whole numbers.	**Step 3** Simplify the sum, if possible.
$\begin{array}{r} 2\frac{3}{10} \\ +\ 3\frac{1}{10} \\ \hline \frac{4}{10} \end{array}$	$\begin{array}{r} 2\frac{3}{10} \\ +\ 3\frac{1}{10} \\ \hline 5\frac{4}{10} \end{array}$	$\begin{array}{r} 2\frac{3}{10} \\ +\ 3\frac{1}{10} \\ \hline 5\frac{4}{10} = 5\frac{2}{5} \end{array}$

Add. $2\frac{5}{6} + 4\frac{1}{4}$

Step 1 Write equivalent fractions for $\frac{1}{6}$ and $\frac{1}{3}$ using the LCD, which is 12.	**Step 2** Add. Simplify the sum, if possible.
$2\frac{5}{6} \rightarrow 2\frac{10}{12}$ $+\ 4\frac{1}{4} \rightarrow +\ 4\frac{3}{12}$	$\begin{array}{r} 2\frac{5}{6} \rightarrow 2\frac{10}{12} \\ +\ 4\frac{1}{4} \rightarrow +\ 4\frac{3}{12} \\ \hline 6\frac{13}{12} = 7\frac{1}{12} \end{array}$

Add. Write each sum in simplest form.

1. $\begin{array}{r} 1\frac{1}{5} \\ +\ 2\frac{2}{5} \\ \hline \end{array}$
2. $\begin{array}{r} 1\frac{1}{8} \\ +\ 1\frac{1}{4} \\ \hline \end{array}$
3. $\begin{array}{r} 5\frac{2}{3} \\ +\ 2\frac{1}{2} \\ \hline \end{array}$
4. $\begin{array}{r} 3\frac{3}{10} \\ +\ 2\frac{1}{5} \\ \hline \end{array}$
5. $\begin{array}{r} 2\frac{5}{6} \\ +\ 1\frac{1}{3} \\ \hline \end{array}$

6. $3\frac{1}{10} + 5\frac{7}{20}$

7. $2\frac{3}{8} + 6\frac{3}{4}$

8. $9\frac{2}{9} + 2\frac{2}{3}$

9. $4\frac{1}{8} + 3\frac{1}{5}$

10. $7\frac{1}{5} + 2\frac{1}{3}$

11. $4\frac{1}{6} + 2\frac{1}{9}$

12. $8\frac{1}{2} + 3\frac{3}{4}$

13. $9\frac{1}{8} + 2\frac{1}{6}$

Name _____ Date _____

Rename Before You Subtract

When subtracting, you may have to rename 1 as an
equivalent fraction.

Subtract. $6 - 1\frac{4}{7}$

Step 1 Rename 6. Use 7 for the denominator.	**Step 2** Subtract the fractions.	**Step 3** Subtract the whole numbers.
$6 = 5 + 1$ $6 = 5 + 1\frac{7}{7}$ $6 = 5\frac{7}{7}$	$\begin{array}{r} 6 = \quad 5\frac{7}{7} \\ -\,1\frac{4}{7} = -\,1\frac{4}{7} \\ \hline \frac{3}{7} \end{array}$	$\begin{array}{r} 6 = \quad 5\frac{7}{7} \\ -\,1\frac{4}{7} = -\,1\frac{4}{7} \\ \hline 4\frac{3}{7} \end{array}$

Subtract. $5\frac{1}{6} - 2\frac{5}{6}$

Step 1 Rename $5\frac{1}{6}$.	**Step 2** Subtract the fractions, then the whole numbers. Simplify.	**Step 3** Use addition to check your answer.
$5\frac{1}{6} = 5 + \frac{1}{6}$ $= 4 + 1 + \frac{1}{6}$ $= 4 + 1\frac{6}{6} + \frac{1}{6}$ $= 4\frac{7}{6}$	$\begin{array}{r} 4\frac{7}{6} = \quad 4\frac{7}{6} \\ -\,2\frac{5}{6} = -\,2\frac{5}{6} \\ \hline 2\frac{2}{6} = 2\frac{1}{3} \end{array}$	$2\frac{1}{3} + 2\frac{5}{6} =$ $2\frac{2}{6} + 2\frac{5}{6} =$ $4\frac{7}{6}$ or $5\frac{1}{6}$

Subtract. Write each difference in simplest form.

1. $\begin{array}{r} 8 \\ -\,2\frac{4}{5} \\ \hline \end{array}$
  2. $\begin{array}{r} 4\frac{1}{4} \\ -\,1\frac{3}{4} \\ \hline \end{array}$
  3. $\begin{array}{r} 4\frac{1}{6} \\ -\,2\frac{2}{3} \\ \hline \end{array}$
  4. $\begin{array}{r} 9 \\ -\,2\frac{1}{8} \\ \hline \end{array}$

5. $4\frac{1}{8} - 3\frac{1}{5}$
  6. $2\frac{3}{8} - \frac{3}{4}$
  7. $5 - 2\frac{2}{6}$
  8. $7 - 5\frac{7}{20}$

_____   _____   _____   _____

9. $6\frac{1}{5} - 2\frac{2}{3}$
  10. $3 - 1\frac{1}{9}$
  11. $8\frac{2}{5} - 3\frac{3}{4}$
  12. $9\frac{1}{4} - 2\frac{3}{4}$

_____   _____   _____   _____

Name _____   Date _____

Subtract Fractions with Unlike Denominators

Subtract. $\frac{1}{4} - \frac{1}{6}$

Different Ways to Subtract Fractions	
You can use any common denominator.	**You can use the least common denominator.**
Use $6 \times 4 = 24$ for the common denominator.	The LCM of 6 and 4 is 12.
$\frac{1 \times 6}{4 \times 6} = \frac{6}{24}$ $\frac{1 \times 4}{6 \times 4} = \frac{4}{24}$	$\frac{1 \times 3}{4 \times 3} = \frac{3}{12}$ $\frac{1 \times 2}{6 \times 2} = \frac{2}{12}$
$\frac{6}{24} - \frac{4}{24} = \frac{2}{24}$	$\frac{3}{12} - \frac{2}{12} = \frac{1}{12}$
$\frac{2}{24} = \frac{1}{12}$ in simplest form	

Subtract. Write the difference in simplest form.

1. $\begin{array}{r} 5\frac{1}{2} \\ -\ 2\frac{1}{3} \\ \hline \end{array}$

2. $\begin{array}{r} \frac{3}{5} \\ -\ \frac{1}{6} \\ \hline \end{array}$

3. $\begin{array}{r} 4\frac{1}{6} \\ -\ 2\frac{2}{3} \\ \hline \end{array}$

4. $\begin{array}{r} \frac{4}{5} \\ -\ \frac{3}{8} \\ \hline \end{array}$

5. $4\frac{5}{8} - 3\frac{1}{6}$

6. $8\frac{3}{4} - 5\frac{1}{6}$

7. $5\frac{2}{3} - 2\frac{1}{4}$

8. $9\frac{8}{9} - 2\frac{1}{3}$

_____   _____   _____   _____

9. $4\frac{3}{4} - 2\frac{1}{5}$

10. $9\frac{5}{6} - 2\frac{7}{10}$

11. $7\frac{7}{8} - 2\frac{3}{8}$

12. $3\frac{3}{10} - 2\frac{1}{6}$

_____   _____   _____   _____

Name _____ Date _____

Subtract Mixed Numbers

Subtract. $13\frac{1}{6} - 6\frac{3}{4} = n$

Step 1 Find the LCD of the fractions.

$$13\frac{1}{6} = 13\frac{\blacksquare}{12}$$
$$-6\frac{3}{4} = -6\frac{\blacksquare}{12}$$

Step 2 Write equivalent fractions.

$$13\frac{1}{6} = 13\frac{2}{12}$$
$$-6\frac{3}{4} = -6\frac{9}{12}$$

Step 3 Rename a mixed number if necessary.

$$13\frac{1}{6} = 13\frac{2}{12} = 12\frac{14}{12}$$
$$-6\frac{3}{4} = -6\frac{9}{12} = -6\frac{9}{12}$$

Step 2 Subtract and simplify.

$$13\frac{1}{6} = 13\frac{2}{12} = 12\frac{14}{12}$$
$$-6\frac{3}{4} = -6\frac{9}{12} = -6\frac{9}{12}$$
$$\overline{\phantom{-6\frac{9}{12}}\ 6\frac{5}{12}}$$

Subtract. Write each difference in simplest form.

1. $\quad 9\frac{1}{7}$
$\quad -2\frac{1}{3}$

2. $\quad 3\frac{1}{3}$
$\quad -1\frac{8}{9}$

3. $\quad 4\frac{1}{6}$
$\quad -2\frac{2}{9}$

4. $\quad 8\frac{3}{8}$
$\quad -2\frac{4}{5}$

5. $14\frac{1}{8} - 3\frac{1}{2}$

6. $18\frac{3}{8} - 15\frac{5}{6}$

7. $10\frac{1}{5} - 2\frac{3}{10}$

8. $8\frac{7}{12} - 2\frac{5}{6}$

9. $12\frac{1}{5} - 3\frac{1}{2}$

10. $4\frac{5}{6} - 3\frac{9}{10}$

11. $9\frac{1}{8} - 7\frac{3}{8}$

12. $3\frac{3}{10} - 2\frac{1}{6}$

Name _____ Date _____

Problem-Solving Application: Use Patterns

Kevin is training for a race. He begins by running half a mile and doubles the distance each day for 5 days and then starts over with the same pattern. How far will he run on the 12th day?

Understand	**What is the question?** How far will he run on the 12th day? **What do you know?** He repeats the same pattern every 5 days. He runs half a mile on the first day and doubles that for 5 days.
Plan	**What can you do to find the answer?** Make a chart to show the pattern.
Solve	The pattern states that he starts with $\frac{1}{2}$ of a mile and doubles his distance each day for 5 days. Then he starts over with the same pattern.

Day	1	2	3	4	5	6	7	8	9	10	11	12	13	14
Distance	$\frac{1}{2}$	1	2	4	8	$\frac{1}{2}$	1	2	4	8	$\frac{1}{2}$	1	2	4

He will run 1 mile on the 12th day.

Look Back	Did you start with $\frac{1}{2}$ and repeat the pattern every 5 days?

Solve.

1. Mark earns $8 an hour. Each year he gets a $0.75 raise. What will be his hourly wage 5 years from now?

Think: How could a chart help you solve this problem? Could you solve this problem using multiplication?

2. Lisa can paint her house in 4 days if she works alone. As the amount of people double, the work time halves. How many hours will it take to finish painting the house if 4 people are working?

Think: Would a chart help solve this problem?

Name _____ Date _____

Model Multiplication of Fractions

Use area to model the product $\frac{5}{6} \times \frac{2}{3}$.

Step 1 Draw a square 1 unit high and 1 unit wide. Divide the height in 6 parts and the width in 3 parts. Label the sides.

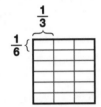

The square is now divided into 18 identical rectangles. Each square represents 18 rectangles.

Step 2 Shade a rectangle that is $\frac{5}{6}$ ft high and $\frac{2}{3}$ ft wide.

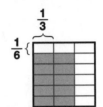

10 rectangles are now shaded.

So, $\frac{5}{6} \times \frac{2}{3} = \frac{10}{18} = \frac{5}{9}$

Write the factors and the product represented by each model.

1.

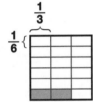

_____

2.

_____

3.

_____

Use models to find each product.

4. $\frac{5}{6} \times \frac{1}{2}$

5. $\frac{1}{6} \times \frac{4}{5}$

_____   _____

6. $\frac{2}{3} \times 9$

7. $\frac{5}{4} \times \frac{2}{3}$

_____   _____

Name _____   Date _____

Multiply Fractions

Find $\frac{3}{4} \times \frac{6}{7}$.

Step 1 Multiply the numerators.
Multiply the denominators.

$$\frac{3}{4} \times \frac{6}{7} = \frac{3 \times 6}{4 \times 7} = \frac{18}{28}$$

Step 2 Simplify the product if necessary.

$$\frac{18}{28} = \frac{2 \times 9}{2 \times 14} = \frac{2}{2} \times \frac{9}{14} = 1 \times \frac{9}{14} = \frac{9}{14}$$

The fraction $\frac{2}{2}$ is equal to 1. When you multiply a number by 1, the product is the number you started with.

Multiply. Write each answer in simplest form.

1. $\frac{3}{5} \times \frac{4}{5}$ _____

2. $\frac{1}{3} \times \frac{1}{2}$ _____

3. $\frac{1}{5} \times \frac{3}{7}$ _____

4. $\frac{1}{2} \times \frac{2}{3}$ _____

5. $\frac{2}{3} \times \frac{1}{4}$ _____

6. $\frac{5}{7} \times \frac{1}{3}$ _____

7. $\frac{4}{9} \times \frac{3}{5}$ _____

8. $\frac{5}{8} \times \frac{2}{7}$ _____

9. $\frac{6}{7} \times \frac{1}{3}$ _____

10. $\frac{2}{5} \times \frac{5}{8}$ _____

11. $\frac{3}{8} \times 2$ _____

12. $\frac{1}{10} \times \frac{2}{5}$ _____

13. $\frac{2}{7} \times 3$ _____

14. $\frac{3}{10} \times \frac{2}{9}$ _____

15. $\frac{1}{6} \times \frac{5}{8}$ _____

16. $\frac{4}{15} \times \frac{5}{8}$ _____

17. $4 \times \frac{3}{4}$ _____

18. $\frac{1}{6} \times \frac{9}{10}$ _____

Name _____   Date _____

Multiply Fractions and Mixed Numbers

Find $\frac{2}{5} \times 2\frac{3}{4}$.

Step 1 Write the mixed number as an improper fraction.	**Step 2** Multiply and simplify.	**Step 3** Write the fraction as a mixed number if necessary.
$2\frac{3}{4} = \frac{4}{4} + \frac{4}{4} + \frac{3}{4} = \frac{11}{4}$	$\frac{2}{5} \times \frac{11}{4} = \frac{22}{20} = \frac{11}{10}$	$\frac{11}{10} = \frac{10}{10} + \frac{1}{10} = 1\frac{1}{10}$

Write each product in simplest form.

1. $1\frac{3}{5} \times \frac{3}{4}$ _____

2. $\frac{1}{3} \times 2\frac{1}{2}$ _____

3. $2\frac{1}{5} \times \frac{3}{7}$ _____

4. $1\frac{3}{7} \times \frac{3}{5}$ _____

5. $3\frac{1}{2} \times \frac{1}{3}$ _____

6. $\frac{1}{3} \times 3\frac{1}{5}$ _____

7. $\frac{1}{2} \times 2\frac{3}{4}$ _____

8. $\frac{1}{4} \times 2\frac{5}{6}$ _____

9. $\frac{1}{8} \times 4\frac{1}{4}$ _____

10. $\frac{5}{6} \times 3\frac{3}{5}$ _____

11. $\frac{3}{4} \times 5\frac{1}{3}$ _____

12. $1\frac{6}{7} \times \frac{1}{3}$ _____

13. $1\frac{2}{3} \times 1\frac{4}{5}$ _____

14. $\frac{2}{3} \times 3\frac{1}{3}$ _____

15. $3\frac{5}{6} \times \frac{2}{5}$ _____

16. $2\frac{2}{3} \times 1\frac{1}{4}$ _____

17. $2\frac{1}{10} \times \frac{2}{7}$ _____

18. $2\frac{1}{3} \times 1\frac{2}{3}$ _____

Name _____   Date _____

Problem-Solving Skill: Choose the Operation

To solve a problem, you need to read the problem carefully
to understand which operation or operations to use.

Look for key words in the problem.	$\frac{2}{3}$ of the 60 people in the band play woodwind instruments. The words "$\frac{2}{3}$ of" indicate that you should multiply.
Sometimes more than one operation is needed.	$\frac{1}{12}$ of the band members play the flute; $\frac{1}{10}$ play the trumpet. How many band members play these two instruments altogether? Multiply to find $\frac{1}{12}$ of 60 and $\frac{1}{10}$ of 60; then add.

Solve.

1. Two tuba players stand 100 yards apart. After each set of steps, the distance between them is $\frac{1}{2}$ the previous distance. How many sets of steps will they take before they are less than 10 yards apart?

Think: When I know the distance apart, how do I find the distance apart after the next set of steps?

_____

2. The marching band stands on the 50-yard line of the football field. After each set of steps, their distance to the goal is $\frac{4}{5}$ of the previous distance. How far do they travel in the 2nd set of steps?

Think: When I know the distance to the goal after a set of steps, how do I find the distance traveled from the last location?

_____

3. How far does the band travel in its 3rd set of steps?

Think: When I know the distance to the goal after a set of steps, how do I find the distance traveled from the last location?

_____

4. $\frac{3}{5}$ of the 60 band members practiced their instruments 1 hour or more last night. $\frac{1}{12}$ of these people practiced 2 hours or more. How many band members practiced 2 hours or more?

Think: When I know the total number, how do I find $\frac{3}{5}$ of the number?

_____

Name _____   Date _____

Divide by a Unit Fraction

Find $4 \div \frac{1}{3}$.

There are 3 thirds in 1 whole. $4 \div \frac{1}{3} = 12$

There are 12 thirds in 4 wholes.   Dividing by $\frac{1}{3}$ is the same as multiplying by 3.

This number strip also shows that $4 \div \frac{1}{3} = 12$.

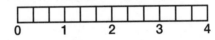

There are 12 thirds in 4.

Check your answer with multiplication: $12 \times \frac{1}{3} = 4$

**Divide. Use a number strip to show the answer.
Check your answer with multiplication.**

1. How many fourths are in 4? _____

2. How many halves are in 6? _____

3. How many fourths are in 2? _____

4. How many fifths are in 3? _____

5. How many sixths are in 1? _____

6. How many fourths are in 5? _____

7. How many halves are in 4? _____

8. How many fifths are in 2? _____

9. How many thirds are in 1? _____

10. How many sixths are in 6? _____

Name _____   Date _____

Divide by a Counting Number

To divide by a counting number, n, you can multiply by the unit fraction $\frac{1}{n}$.

Divide. $4\frac{2}{3} \div 2$

Step 1 Write the mixed number as a fraction.	**Step 2** Divide by multiplying by a unit fraction.	**Step 3** Simplify.
$4\frac{2}{3} = \frac{14}{3}$	$\frac{14}{3} \div 2 = \frac{14}{3} \times \frac{1}{2} = \frac{14}{6}$	$\frac{14}{6} = 2\frac{2}{6} = 2\frac{1}{3}$

Divide by multiplying by a unit fraction. Simplify your answer.

1. $2 \div 5$ _____

2. $5 \div 3$ _____

3. $\frac{4}{5} \div 2$ _____

4. $\frac{3}{7} \div 3$ _____

5. $1\frac{1}{3} \div 2$ _____

6. $\frac{2}{5} \div 4$ _____

7. $1\frac{1}{2} \div 5$ _____

8. $5 \div 4$ _____

9. $\frac{3}{5} \div 2$ _____

10. $2\frac{1}{2} \div 7$ _____

11. $1\frac{2}{3} \div 5$ _____

12. $5 \div 7$ _____

13. $2\frac{1}{7} \div 2$ _____

14. $\frac{7}{8} \div 3$ _____

15. $1\frac{1}{4} \div 5$ _____

16. $\frac{8}{3} \div 2$ _____

17. $\frac{7}{5} \div 3$ _____

18. $4\frac{2}{3} \div 2$ _____

Name _____ Date _____

Problem-Solving Strategy: Solve a Simpler Problem

Simplifying the facts can help you solve a problem.

ABC Storage stores old materials for companies in file boxes. The weight of an old file box is $4\frac{2}{3}$ oz. New file boxes weigh $6\frac{1}{6}$ oz. What will be the total increase in the weight of 60,000 boxes if all the old boxes are replaced with new boxes?

How can you find the answer? Think of a simpler problem.

The increase in each box's weight was $6\frac{1}{6}$ oz. $- 4\frac{2}{3}$ oz. $= 1\frac{1}{2}$ oz.

Multiply by the number of boxes. $60,000 \times 1\frac{1}{2} = 90,000$ oz.

The weight of the boxes will increase by 90,000 ounces.

Solve each problem, using the Solve a Simpler Problem strategy.

1. ABC Storage is also looking at lightweight boxes which weigh $3\frac{1}{2}$ ounces. What will be the decrease in the total weight of the boxes if the lightweight boxes are used?

   Think: How is the decrease in the weight of one box related to the total decrease in weight?

2. In 2002, the company stores 45,000 tons of material. It hopes to increase that amount by $\frac{1}{5}$ each year. If they are able to do this, how many tons of material will they store in 2004?

   Think: How much will the tonnage increase by 2003? What is the total tonnage by 2003?

3. The company spent $10,000 on advertising in 2000. Each year it has decreased that amount by $\frac{1}{10}$. How much did it spend on advertising in 2002?

   Think: How much did the advertising budget decrease in 2001? What was the amount spent that year?

4. ABC Storage invested in a company whose shares rose from $15\frac{1}{2}$ to $21\frac{7}{8}$. If they own 40,000 shares, what was the change in the shares' value?

   Think: How is the increase in the price of one share related to the increase in the total value?

Name _____   Date _____

Divide by a Fraction

Divide. $4 \div \frac{2}{3}$

Step 1 Find the reciprocal of the divisor.

The reciprocal of $\frac{2}{3}$ is $\frac{3}{2}$.

Step 2 Multiply by the reciprocal of the divisor.

$4 \div \frac{2}{3} = 4 \times \frac{3}{2} = \frac{4}{1} \times \frac{3}{2} = \frac{12}{2} = 6$

Divide. Multiply by the reciprocal of the divisor. Write answers in simplest form.

1. $\frac{1}{6} \div \frac{5}{3}$ _____

2. $\frac{1}{3} \div 1\frac{2}{3}$ _____

3. $\frac{4}{11} \div \frac{1}{2}$ _____

4. $1\frac{4}{5} \div \frac{1}{3}$ _____

5. $\frac{1}{4} \div \frac{1}{8}$ _____

6. $1\frac{3}{5} \div 1\frac{1}{7}$ _____

7. $\frac{2}{9} \div \frac{3}{9}$ _____

8. $\frac{7}{10} \div 1\frac{2}{5}$ _____

9. $1\frac{3}{11} \div 1\frac{1}{6}$ _____

10. $\frac{2}{5} \div \frac{4}{6}$ _____

11. $\frac{1}{2} \div \frac{3}{5}$ _____

12. $\frac{2}{7} \div \frac{4}{7}$ _____

13. $\frac{3}{5} \div \frac{3}{4}$ _____

14. $1\frac{5}{6} \div \frac{7}{6}$ _____

15. $\frac{2}{3} \div \frac{2}{5}$ _____

16. $3\frac{5}{9} \div \frac{5}{6}$ _____

17. $\frac{1}{7} \div \frac{2}{5}$ _____

18. $3\frac{7}{8} \div \frac{1}{2}$ _____

Name _____ Date _____

Divide With Mixed Numbers

Find $1\frac{2}{3} \div 1\frac{3}{7}$.

Step 1 Write the mixed numbers as improper fractions.

$1\frac{2}{3} \div 1\frac{3}{7} = \frac{5}{3} \div \frac{10}{7}$

Step 2 Write the reciprocal of the divisor.

$\frac{5}{3} \div \frac{10}{7} = \frac{5}{3} \times \frac{7}{10}$

Step 3 Find the prime factorization of the numerator and denominator.

$\frac{5}{3} \times \frac{7}{10} = \frac{5 \times 7}{3 \times 10} = \frac{\overset{1}{\cancel{5}} \times 7}{3 \times 2 \times \underset{1}{\cancel{5}}}$

Step 4 Write the answer in simplest form.

$\frac{1 \times 7}{3 \times 2 \times 1} = \frac{7}{6} = 1\frac{1}{6}$

Write each quotient in simplest form.

1. $\frac{2}{3} \div 1\frac{2}{3}$ _____

2. $\frac{5}{6} \div 2\frac{5}{6}$ _____

3. $1\frac{1}{7} \div 1\frac{2}{7}$ _____

4. $\frac{1}{4} \div 5\frac{1}{2}$ _____

5. $\frac{1}{8} \div 2\frac{3}{8}$ _____

6. $2\frac{2}{3} \div 1\frac{1}{3}$ _____

7. $1\frac{2}{5} \div 2\frac{3}{5}$ _____

8. $\frac{2}{3} \div 2\frac{1}{6}$ _____

9. $2\frac{1}{3} \div 2\frac{1}{2}$ _____

10. $2\frac{1}{3} \div 1\frac{1}{4}$ _____

11. $1\frac{1}{4} \div 1\frac{2}{3}$ _____

12. $3\frac{1}{2} \div 1\frac{1}{4}$ _____

13. $3\frac{1}{8} \div \frac{5}{7}$ _____

14. $2\frac{4}{7} \div 1\frac{13}{14}$ _____

15. $3\frac{4}{5} \div 1\frac{1}{3}$ _____

Name _____ Date _____

Problem-Solving Application: Using Circle Graphs

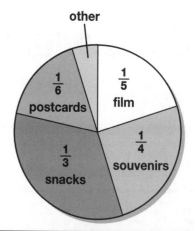

The circle graph shows how Ramon spent his money on summer vacation. If he spent $12 on film, how much did he spend on the whole vacation?

Understand	**What is the question?** How much money did Ramon spend on vacation? **What do you know?** He spent $12 on film. He spent $\frac{1}{5}$ of his money on film.
Plan	**What can you do to find the answer?** Divide the amount of money spent on film by the fraction of the money spent on film.
Solve	$12 \div \frac{1}{5} = \$60$. Ramon spent $60 on vacation.
Look Back	Is $60 a reasonable amount of money to take on vacation?

Solve. Use the circle graph.

1. If $\frac{1}{3}$ of Ramon's money came from his pet-sitting service, and half of that came from watching the Ryan's dog, how much came from watching the Ryan's dog?

Think: Do you need to multiply or divide to solve this problem?

2. What fraction of Ramon's money was spent on something other than film, souvenirs, snacks and postcards?

Think: What is the sum of all the fractions in the circle graph?

3. How much money did Ramon spend on postcards and souvenirs altogether?

Think: What operations are needed?

4. Ramon spent $\frac{1}{4}$ of his snack money on chips and soda and the rest on healthy snacks. How much did Ramon spend on healthy snacks?

Think: What operations are needed?

Name _____   Date _____

Multiply Whole Numbers and Decimals

Multiply $9 \times 0.3 = n$

Different Ways to Multiply Whole Numbers and Decimals

You can write the factors as fractions.

Step 1 Write each factor as a fraction.	**Step 2** Multiply.	**Step 3** Simplify.
$9 \times 0.3 = \frac{9}{1} \times \frac{3}{10}$	$\frac{9}{1} \times \frac{3}{10} = \frac{27}{10}$	$2\frac{7}{10}$ or 2.7

You can multiply and place the decimal point.

Step 1 Multiply the factors as if they were whole numbers.	**Step 2** Place a decimal point in the product.
$\begin{array}{r} 0.3 \\ \times\ 9 \\ \hline 27 \end{array}$	$\begin{array}{r} 0.3 \\ \times\ 9 \\ \hline 2.7 \end{array}$ ← 1 decimal place ← +0 decimal places ← 1 decimal place The number of decimal places in the product must equal the total number of decimal places in the factors.

Find each product.

1. 8×0.4 **2.** 3×0.6 **3.** 9×0.2 **4.** 5×0.6

_____   _____   _____   _____

5. 9×4.5 **6.** 2×8.3 **7.** 4×9.3 **8.** 2×5.6

_____   _____   _____   _____

9. 5×4.22 **10.** 6×9.49 **11.** 7×4.61 **12.** 3×4.93

_____   _____   _____   _____

Name _____ Date _____

Estimate Products

Estimate the product. 872 × 0.49

Step 1 Round each factor.	**Step 2** Multiply the rounded factors as if they were whole numbers.	**Step 3** Place a decimal point in the estimated product.
872 rounds to 900 × 0.49 rounds to × 0.5	900 × 0.5 ——— 4500	900 ← 0 decimal places × 0.5 ←+1 decimal place ——— 450.0 ← 1 decimal place

Estimate each product by rounding each factor.

1. 9.438
    × 22

2. 5.872
    × 48

3.   493
    × 0.81

4.   735
    × 0.56

5.   582
    × 5.3

6.   239
    × 7.7

7. 42 × 3.14 _____

8. 92 × 7.92 _____

9. 22 × 0.82 _____

10. 74 × 0.38 _____

11. 6.4 × 471 _____

12. 8.5 × 299 _____

Name _____   Date _____

Multiply Decimals

Multiply. 0.4 × 0.7

Different Ways to Multiply Decimals

You can write the factors as fractions.

Step 1 Write each factor as a fraction	**Step 2** Multiply and simplify.

$$0.4 \times 0.7 = \frac{4}{10} \times \frac{7}{10}$$

$$\frac{4}{10} \times \frac{7}{10} = \frac{28}{100} = 0.28$$

You can multiply and place the decimal point.

Step 1 Multiply the factors disregarding the decimal points.	**Step 2** Place the decimal point.

$$\begin{array}{r} 0.4 \\ \times\ 0.7 \\ \hline 28 \end{array}$$

$$\begin{array}{r} 0.4 \leftarrow \quad \text{1 decimal place} \\ \times\ 0.7 \leftarrow +\text{1 decimal place} \\ \hline 0.28 \leftarrow \quad \text{2 decimal places} \end{array}$$

The number of decimal places in the product must equal the total number of decimal places in the factors.

Multiply.

1. 5 × 0.45

_____

2. 8 × 0.93

_____

3. 7 × 0.44

_____

4. 0.4 × 0.9

_____

5. 0.2 × 0.8

_____

6. 0.9 × 0.1

_____

7. 0.5 × 0.49

_____

8. 0.3 × 0.59

_____

9. 0.45 × 0.8

_____

10. 0.5 × 0.88

_____

11. 8.39 × 1.5

_____

12. 4.22 × 4.8

_____

Name _____ Date _____

Zeros in the Product

Find 0.16 × 0.4

Step 1 Multiply the factors as if they were whole numbers.	**Step 2** Count the number of decimal places needed for the product.	**Step 3** Write as many zeros as you need to place the decimal point correctly.
0.16 × 0.4 ── 64	0.16 ← 2 decimal places × 0.4 ← +1 decimal place ── 0.064 ← 3 decimal places	0.16 × 0.4 ── 0.064

Multiply. Write as many zeros as you need to place the decimal point correctly.

1.   0.3
    × 0.3

2.   0.1
    × 0.9

3.   0.3
    × 0.2

4.   0.27
    × 0.3

5.   0.31
    × 0.3

6.   0.18
    × 0.3

7. 0.7 × 0.13 _____

8. 0.03 × 0.5 _____

9. 0.05 × 0.08 _____

10. 0.45 × 0.3 _____

11. 0.28 × 0.02 _____

12. 0.004 × 0.4 _____

Name _____ Date _____

Problem-Solving Strategy: Find a Pattern

Tyrone opened a savings account with $15.00 and then made equal deposits each month. After a month, his balance was $18.50; after two months, it was $22.00; and after three months, it was $25.50. What will Tyrone's balance likely be after 4 months?

Understand

- What is the question?

  What will Tyrone's balance be after 4 months?

- What do you know?

  He began with $15.00. He made equal deposits each month.

Plan/Solve

- How can you find the answer?

  Make a table. Look for a pattern and then use the pattern.

Month	Balance
0	$15.00
1	$18.50
2	$22.00
3	$25.50
4	$29.00

The balance increases by $3.50 each month.

Use the pattern to find the balance after 4 months.

It will be $29.00 after 4 months.

Solve each problem, using the Find a Pattern strategy.

1. Gary's goal is to double his earnings each week. If he makes $5.00 the first week, how much will he likely make in the 4th week? the 8th week?

   Think: Is there a pattern to how much his salary increases every week?

2. Jo's pea plant is 4.3 cm tall. After 5 days, it is 5.5 cm tall, after 10 days it is 6.7 cm tall, and after 15 days it is 7.9 cm tall. How tall will it likely be after 30 days?

   Think: Is there a pattern you can use to find the plant's height after 30 days?

3. At birth, a kitten weighed 1.5 kg. After 1 month, it weighed 1.9 kg. After 2 months, it weighed 2.3 kg. If this pattern continues, how much will the kitten likely weigh after 6 months?

   Think: Is there a pattern you can use to find the kitten's weight after 6 months?

4. Some groceries totaled $75.39 before the plums were scanned. After scanning one plum, the total was $75.74. After scanning another plum, it was $76.09. What will the total likely be after 5 plums are scanned?

   Think: Is there a pattern that you can use to find the total cost of the groceries?

Name _____   Date _____

Multiply and Divide Decimals by Powers of 10

When you multiply or divide a number by 10^n, the exponent tells you how many places to move the decimal point.

Find 0.093×10^2.	Find $5.28 \div 10^3$.
$0.093 \times 10^2 = 9.3$	$5.28 \div 10^3 = 0.00528$
The decimal point moves 2 places to the right.	The decimal point moves 3 places to the left.
Eliminate the zeros that do not affect the value of the product.	Add zeros as necessary to place the decimal point.

Multiply or divide.

1. 8.3×10^2 **2.** $9.43 \div 10^0$ **3.** 0.04×10^3 **4.** $0.35 \div 10^2$

_____   _____   _____   _____

5. $9.4 \div 1{,}000$ **6.** 7.63×10^2 **7.** $5.8 \div 1{,}000$ **8.** 4.22×10^1

_____   _____   _____   _____

9. $8.45 \div 100$ **10.** 5.33×100 **11.** $8.4 \div 10^3$ **12.** 2.05×10^2

_____   _____   _____   _____

13. $0.04 \div 10$ **14.** $0.03 \times 1{,}000$ **15.** 9.4×10^2 **16.** $0.33 \div 10^2$

_____   _____   _____   _____

Name _____ Date _____

Divide a Decimal by a Whole Number

Divide. 8.4 ÷ 6 = *n*

Different Ways to Divide a Decimal by a Whole Number

You can use fractions.

Step 1 Write the dividend and the divisor as fractions.	**Step 2** Multiply the dividend by the reciprocal of the divisor.	**Step 3** Write the quotient as a decimal.
$\frac{84}{10} \div \frac{6}{1}$	$\frac{84}{10} \times \frac{1}{6} = \frac{84}{60}$	$\frac{84}{60} = \frac{14}{10} = 1.4$

You can divide and place the decimal point in the quotient.

Step 1 Divide disregarding the decimal point.	**Step 2** Place a decimal point in the quotient directly above the decimal point in the dividend.
1 4 6)8.4 −6 2 4 −2 4 0	1.4 6)8.4 −6 2 4 −2 4 0 Check: 1.4 × 6 = 8.4

Divide and check.

1. 3)2.7

2. 8)6.4

3. 6)3.66

4. 8)14.4

5. 7)0.98

6. 4)65.6

7. 84.3 ÷ 3 _____

8. 2.25 ÷ 5 _____

9. 39.6 ÷ 6 _____

10. 0.84 ÷ 6 _____

11. 0.48 ÷ 3 _____

12. .084 ÷ 2 _____

Name _____ Date _____

Problem-Solving Skill: Interpret Remainders

When you solve a problem that has a remainder, you need to decide what to do with the remainder.

Sometimes you use the remainder to decide on the answer. If each cookie sheet holds 9 cookies, how many sheets will you have to use to make 50 cookies?	$$\begin{array}{r} 5\ R5 \\ 9\overline{)50} \\ -45 \\ \hline 5 \end{array}$$	There will be 5 full cookie sheets. Another one will be needed for the 5 extra cookies. So 6 cookie sheets are needed in all.
Sometimes you write the remainder as a fraction. If you divide 9 cups of flour evenly into 4 bowls, how much will be in each bowl?	$$\begin{array}{r} 2\ R1 \\ 4\overline{)9} \\ -8 \\ \hline 1 \end{array}$$	$= 2\frac{1}{4}$ There will be $2\frac{1}{4}$ cups of flour in each bowl.
Sometimes you write the remainder as a decimal. If 4 bags of chocolate chips cost $5.00, what is the price per bag?	$$\begin{array}{r} 1.25 \\ 4\overline{)5.00} \\ -4 \\ \hline 1\,0 \\ -\ 8 \\ \hline 20 \\ -20 \\ \hline 0 \end{array}$$	Each bag of chocolate chips costs $1.25

Solve.

1. How many 4-tablespoon scoops of sugar can be taken from a bowl holding 58 tablespoons of sugar?

   Think: Can you take part of a scoop?

   _____

2. Gretl is selling tarts. If 8 tarts sell for $12.00, how much is each tart?

   Think: How many dollars and cents does each pie cost?

   _____

3. If Stacey splits a dozen cookies among her 5 teachers, how many whole cookies will each teacher get?

   _____

4. Rosa made 3 batches of brownies. If she used a total of 4 cups of flour, how much flour was used for each batch?

   _____

Name _____ Date _____

Write Zeros in the Dividend

Find 6.2 ÷ 4.

Step 1 Divide as though the dividend were a whole number.	**Step 2** To continue the division, write a 0 in the hundredths place.	**Step 3** Place the decimal point in the quotient directly above its place in the dividend.
$$\begin{array}{r} 1\,5 \\ 4\overline{)6.2} \\ -4 \\ \hline 2\,2 \\ -2\,0 \\ \hline 2 \end{array}$$	$$\begin{array}{r} 1\,55 \\ 4\overline{)6.20} \\ -4 \\ \hline 2\,2 \\ -2\,0 \\ \hline 20 \\ -20 \\ \hline 0 \end{array}$$	$$\begin{array}{r} 1.55 \\ 4\overline{)6.20} \\ -4 \\ \hline 2\,2 \\ -2\,0 \\ \hline 20 \\ -20 \\ \hline 0 \end{array}$$

Divide and check.

1. $4\overline{)2.5}$

2. $5\overline{)3.9}$

3. $4\overline{)8.5}$

4. $6\overline{)8.1}$

5. $5\overline{)32}$

6. $2\overline{)4.1}$

7. $5\overline{)4.6}$

8. $4\overline{)33}$

9. $2\overline{)54.35}$

10. $10\overline{)355}$

11. $11\overline{)156.2}$

12. $9\overline{)31.95}$

Name _____   Date _____

Divide by a Decimal

Divide. $0.8\overline{)76}$

Step 1 To change the divisor to a whole number, multiply by 10.	**Step 2** Multiply the dividend by the same number, 10, so the quotient will stay the same.	**Step 3** Complete the division.
$0.8 \times 10 = 8$ $8\overline{)76}$	$76 \times 10 = 760$ $8\overline{)760}$	$\begin{array}{r} 95 \\ 8\overline{)760} \\ -72 \\ \hline 40 \\ -40 \\ \hline 0 \end{array}$

Divide and check.

1. $2.4\overline{)48}$

2. $1.5\overline{)60}$

3. $0.3\overline{)27}$

4. $0.8\overline{)72}$

5. $0.3\overline{)36}$

6. $0.5\overline{)40}$

7. $4.5\overline{)90}$

8. $2.6\overline{)39}$

9. $3.5\overline{)77}$

10. $2.5\overline{)7}$

11. $0.6\overline{)3}$

12. $4.5\overline{)450}$

Name _____ Date _____

Divide a Decimal by a Decimal

Divide. 16.52 ÷ 3.5

Step 1 Multiply both the divisor and the dividend by 10 to simplify the problem.

$$3.5 \overline{)16.52}$$

Step 2 Since there are not enough hundreds or tens to divide, begin dividing in the ones place.

$$\begin{array}{r} 4 \\ 35 \overline{)165.2} \\ -140 \\ \hline 25 \end{array}$$

Step 3 Bring down the tenths. Divide the tenths.

$$\begin{array}{r} 4\,7 \\ 35 \overline{)165.2} \\ -140 \\ \hline 25\,2 \\ -24\,5 \\ \hline 7 \end{array}$$

Step 4 Write a zero after the final digit of the dividend. Place a decimal point in the quotient directly over the decimal point in the dividend.

$$\begin{array}{r} 4.72 \\ 35 \overline{)165.20} \\ -140 \\ \hline 25\,2 \\ -24\,5 \\ \hline 70 \\ -70 \\ \hline 0 \end{array}$$

Divide and check.

1. $0.9 \overline{)1.8}$

2. $0.8 \overline{)4.8}$

3. $2.4 \overline{)8.76}$

4. $0.6 \overline{)8.4}$

5. $0.7 \overline{)2.457}$

6. $3.4 \overline{)12.92}$

7. $5.3 \overline{)24.38}$

8. $3.5 \overline{)17.85}$

9. $0.4 \overline{)0.085}$

Name _____   Date _____

Problem-Solving Application:
Use Formulas

Quincy's backyard is a rectangle. A border of
flowers divides the rectangle into two equal
rectangular halves. If each half of the backyard
is 25 feet wide and has an area of 925 ft^2,
what is the length of each half?

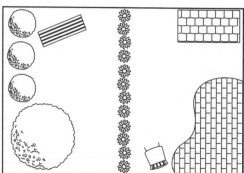

Understand	**Plan**	**Solve**	**Look Back**
• What is the question? What is the length of each half of the backyard? • What do you know? Each half is a rectangle with area 925 ft^2 and width 25 ft.	• What can you do to find the answer? Use the formula for finding the area of a rectangle. Area = length × width = $l \times w$	• Substitute the values you know into the formula. Use l to represent the length of the rectangle. $925 = l \times 25$ $925 \div 25 = l$ The length of each half of the backyard is 37 ft.	• Look back at the question. Is your answer reasonable? In the diagram, the length is slightly longer than the width, so 37 ft is reasonable.

Solve.

1. Ophelia's backyard is a square with
   sides 15 meters long. A rock wall
   divides the backyard into two
   rectangular portions. One portion has
   width 3 meters. What is the area of
   that portion?

    How can you use the side
   lengths of a rectangle to
   find its area?

2. Each half of Charles' rectangular
   backyard is a square with perimeter
   of 58 yards. How long is each side of
   the squares?

    What formula shows how
   the side length of a square
   is related to its perimeter?

   _____

   _____

Name _____ Date _____

Points, Lines, and Rays

The Language of Geometry

A **point** is a location in space that has no length, width, or height.

$\bullet$
A

Read: point A

Write: • A

A **line** is a straight, continuous, and unending path made up of a collection of points in a plane.

A   B

Read: line AB or line BA

Write: $\overleftrightarrow{AB}$ or $\overleftrightarrow{BA}$

A **line segment** is the part of a line between any two points on the line, called endpoints.

A   B

Read: line segment AB or line segment BA

Write: $\overline{AB}$ or $\overline{BA}$

A **ray** is a part of a line made up of one endpoint and all the points on one side of it.

R   P

Read: ray RP

Write: $\overrightarrow{RP}$

A **plane** is a flat surface made up of a continuous and unending collection of points.

Read: plane ABC

Name each figure.

1. $\bullet$
Y

_____

2.
T   P

_____

3.
M   N

_____

4.
W   N

_____

5.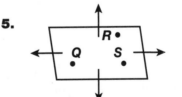

_____

6.
T   G

_____

Draw and label a picture for each description.

7. $\overrightarrow{AB}$

8. Plane PQR

9. Point X

10. $\overline{PY} \perp \overline{CD}$

11. $\overrightarrow{ST}$

12. $\overrightarrow{JK} \parallel \overrightarrow{TU}$

13. $\overline{FG}$

14. $\overleftrightarrow{MN}$

Name _____ Date _____

Measure and Draw Angles

A protractor is a tool that is used to measure angles in degrees.
Follow these steps to measure ∠HNR.

Step 1 Place the center mark of the protractor on the vertex, *N*.

Step 2 Align the 0° mark of one of the protractor scales with one ray of the angle to be measured.

Step 3 Find where the other ray passes through the same scale. Read the measure of the angle on that scale.

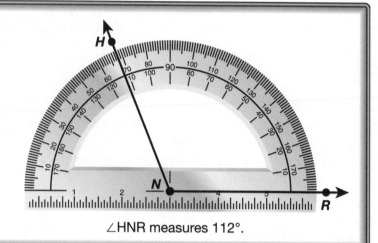

∠HNR measures 112°.

Use symbols to name each angle three different ways.

1.

2.

3.

4.

_____   _____   _____   _____

_____   _____   _____   _____

_____   _____   _____   _____

Classify each angle as *acute*, *obtuse*, *straight* or *right*.

5.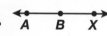

6.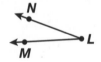

7.

8.

_____   _____   _____   _____

Use a protractor to draw an angle having each measure.
Then classify the angle as *right*, *acute*, *obtuse* or *straight*.

9. 23°   10. 142°   11. 90°   12. 10°

_____   _____   _____   _____

Name _____   Date _____

Triangles

Different Ways to Classify Triangles

You can classify triangles by the length of their sides.

equilateral triangle

all sides are the same length

isosceles triangle

at least two sides are the same length

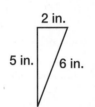

scalene triangle

no sides are the same length

You can classify triangles by their angle measures. The sum of the angle measures in any triangle is 180°.

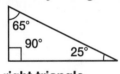

right triangle

one right angle

acute triangle

all acute angles

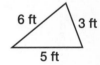

obtuse triangle

one obtuse angle

Classify each triangle in two ways.

1.

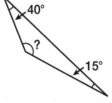

2.

3.

4.

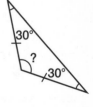

_____   _____   _____   _____

_____   _____   _____   _____

Find each missing angle measure. Then classify each triangle in two ways.

5. 40° ? 15°

6. 45° ?

7. ? 30° 60°

8. 30° ? 30°

_____   _____   _____   _____

Name _____ Date _____

Congruence

┌───┐
Different Ways to Check for Congruence

You can use tracing. If you trace rectangle *ABCD* and place it on top of rectangle *WXYZ*, you will find that the rectangles are identical.

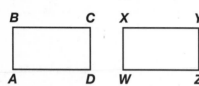

ABCD ≅ *WXYZ*

You can use a ruler and a protractor.

In a rectangle, 2 pairs of sides are congruent, and all the angles are congruent. The marks indicate congruent sides and congruent angles.
└───┘

Trace these figures. Mark the sides and angles that appear to be congruent.

1.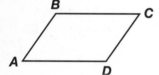

2.

3.

Use a ruler to measure the sides and a protractor to measure the angles of each figure. Mark and name the congruent sides and congruent angles.

4.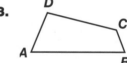

5.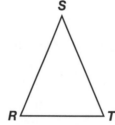

6.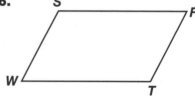

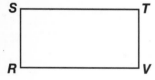

_____ _____ _____

_____ _____ _____

Name _____ Date _____

Quadrilaterals

Classifying Quadrilaterals

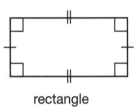

rectangle
opposite sides congruent
four right angles

square
four congruent sides
four right angles

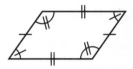

parallelogram
opposite sides congruent
and parallel

rhombus
four congruent sides
opposite sides parallel

trapezoid
one pair of parallel sides

Classify each figure in as many ways as possible. Then find the missing angle measures.

1.
100°

2.
60°

3.
70°

4.

_____   _____   _____   _____

_____   _____   _____   _____

_____   _____   _____   _____

Use the figure to answer each question.

5. Name two congruent triangles.

_____

6. Name a quadrilateral that is not a parallelogram.

_____

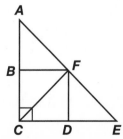

Name _____   Date _____

Problem-Solving Strategy: Solve a Simpler Problem

Sometimes you can solve a problem by solving a simpler problem.

How many triangular pieces were used to make these 3 kites?

Understand	**What is the question?** How many triangular pieces are in the 3 kites? **What do you know?** Each kite is made up of triangles.
Plan	**How can you find the answer?** Count the number of triangles in one kite, then multiply by the number of kites.
Solve	There are 8 triangles per kite, and 3 kites, so there are 24 triangles altogether.
Look Back	**Is your answer reasonable? Tell why.**

Solve each problem by solving a simpler problem.

1. Look at the kite. How many triangles can you find in this figure?

Think: How many sizes of triangles can you find in the figure?

_____

2. How many triangles can you find in this kite?

Think: How does the answer to Problem 1 help with this problem?

_____

3. How many squares can you find in this figure?

Think: How many sizes of squares can you find in the figure?

_____

4. How many squares can you find in this figure?

Think: How does the answer to Problem 3 help with this problem?

_____

Name _____ Date _____

Circles and Angles

A circle is the set of all points in a plane that are the same distance from a given point called the **center**.

- Point *A* is the **center**.
- Line segment *AD* is a **radius**.
- Line segment *BC* is a **diameter**.
- ∠*DAB* is a **central angle**.
- Line segment *DE* is a **chord**.

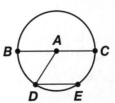

Use symbols to identify the following parts of this circle.

1. radii

_____

2. chords

_____

3. central angles

_____

4. diameter

_____

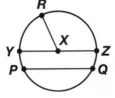

Classify each figure as a *radius*, *diameter*, *chord* or *central angle*. Indicate if more than one term applies.

5. $\overline{MO}$

_____

_____

6. ∠*RNM*

_____

_____

7. $\overline{NR}$

_____

_____

8. $\overline{NO}$

_____

_____

9. ∠*MNO*

_____

_____

10. $\overline{PQ}$

_____

_____

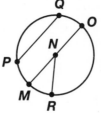

On a separate sheet of paper, construct a circle that contains all of the following:

11. Radius *FG*

12. Diameter *FH*

13. Chord *CD*

Name _____ Date _____

Parallel and Perpendicular Lines

> A compass and straightedge can be used to construct perpendicular
> and parallel lines.
>
> - **Parallel** lines never intersect. They are always the same distance
>   from each other.
> - **Perpendicular** lines intersect at right angles.

Use a compass and a straightedge for Exercises 1–4.

1. Draw a line *x*. Label a point *Z* that is not on line *x*.
   Construct line *y* that is parallel to line *x* and passes through point *Z*.

2. Draw and label line *t*. Label a point *S* that is not on line *t*.
   Construct line *r* perpendicular to line *t* that passes through point *S*.

3. Construct a parallelogram and label it *RSTU*.

4. Construct a rectangle and label it *LMNP*.

Name _____ Date _____

Triangles and Rectangles

You can construct triangles and rectangles with a compass and straightedge.

Construct triangle *ABC* congruent to equilateral triangle *RST*.

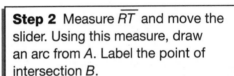

Step 1 Draw a line. Mark a point on the line. Label the point *A*.

Step 2 Measure $\overline{RT}$ and move the slider. Using this measure, draw an arc from *A*. Label the point of intersection *B*.

Step 3 Without changing the compass measure, draw an arc from point *A* and an arc from point *B*. Label the point of intersection *C*.

Step 4 Use a straightedge to draw $\overline{AC}$ and $\overline{BC}$.

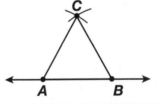

Complete each construction.

1. Construct triangle *MNO* congruent to equilateral triangle *JKL*.

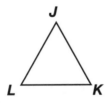

2. Construct square *ABCD* congruent to square *WXYZ*.

Name _____ Date _____

Symmetry

A figure has **rotational symmetry** if you can turn it less than a full turn about a fixed point, and the figure looks exactly as it did before the turn. 180°	A figure has **line symmetry** if it can be folded in half and the two halves are congruent. The fold is a line of symmetry.

Trace the figure and turn it. Then, for each figure, write *yes* or *no* to tell if it has rotational symmetry. If it does, tell how many degrees you turned it.

1.

_____

2.

_____

3.

_____

Trace each figure and fold it. Then, for each figure, write *yes* or *no* to tell if it has line symmetry. If it does, write the number of lines of symmetry that it has.

4.

_____

5.

_____

6.

_____

Use a compass, a protractor and another sheet of paper to draw these figures.

7. A figure with one line of symmetry

8. A figure with rotational symmetry

9. A figure with 4 lines of symmetry

Name _____ Date _____

Problem-Solving Skill: Visual Thinking

When solving a problem, it can help if you visualize the solution and work backward.

The figure shown is made up of 10 toothpicks arranged to make 3 small squares.

Problem: Move 2 toothpicks so 2 congruent squares that do not share a side remain.

Sometimes you can visualize a problem. Visualize 2 squares made of toothpicks. Squares have 4 sides, so 2 squares would use 8 toothpicks.

Then you can manipulate a model. If you remove the two middle horizontal toothpicks, you are left with two squares which do not share a side.

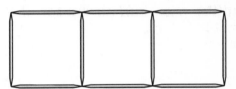

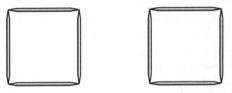

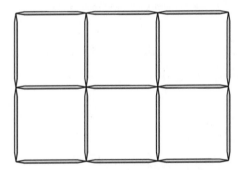

Solve.

1. How can you remove three toothpicks to leave four squares?

> Think: Can the squares share sides?

_____

2. How can you remove two toothpicks and leave 5 squares?

> Think: Can the squares share sides?

_____

3. How many toothpicks would you need to remove to form 3 rectangles?

> Think: Can the rectangles share sides?

_____

4. How can you remove exactly four toothpicks to form 3 squares?

> Think: Do the squares have to be the same size?

_____

Name _____ Date _____

Perimeter and Area of Complex Figures

Find the area and perimeter of the figure.

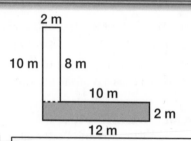

Find the area of the figure.

Step 1 Divide the figure into simple figures. For example, draw a line that divides the figure into two rectangles.

Step 2 Use formulas to find the area of each figure.

Rectangle 1: $8 \times 2 = 16 \text{ m}^2$
Rectangle 2: $12 \times 2 = 24 \text{ m}^2$

Step 3 Find the sum of the areas.

$A = 16 \text{ m}^2 + 24 \text{ m}^2 = 40 \text{ m}^2$

Find the perimeter of the figure.

Find the perimeter by finding the sum of the lengths of the sides.

$P = 10 \text{ m} + 12 \text{ m} + 2 \text{ m} + 10 \text{ m} + 8 \text{ m} + 2 \text{ m} = 44 \text{ m}$

Find the perimeter and area of each figure.

1.

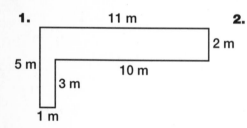

_____

_____

2.

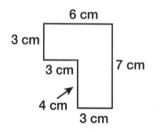
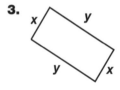

_____

_____

3.

_____

_____

Algebra • Expressions

Write an expression to represent the perimeter of each figure.

4.

_____

5.

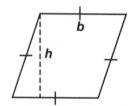

_____

6.

_____

Name _____ Date _____

Find the Area of a Parallelogram

The formula for the area of a parallelogram is $A = bh$.

$A = bh$
$A = 5\,m \times 6\,m$
$A = 30\,m^2$

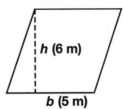

h (6 m)

b (5 m)

Find the area of each figure.

1.

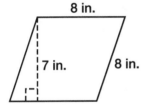

8 in.

7 in.   8 in.

2.

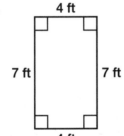

4 ft

7 ft   7 ft

4 ft

3.

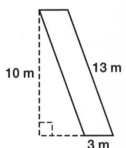

10 m   13 m

3 m

_____   _____   _____

4.

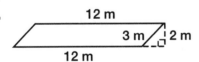

12 m

3 m   2 m

12 m

5.

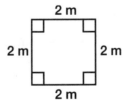

2 m

2 m   2 m

2 m

6.

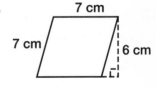

7 cm

7 cm   6 cm

_____   _____   _____

Name _____   Date _____

Find the Area of a Triangle

The formula for finding the area of a triangle is $A = \frac{1}{2}bh$ or $A = \frac{bh}{2}$.

Find the area of the triangle.

$A = \frac{bh}{2}$

$A = \frac{12\text{ m} \times 8\text{ m}}{2} = \frac{96\text{ m}^2}{2} = 48\text{ m}^2$

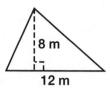
8 m
12 m

Find the area of each triangle.

1.

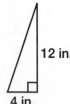
12 in.
4 in.

_____

2.

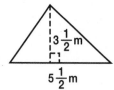
$3\frac{1}{2}$ m
$5\frac{1}{2}$ m

_____

3.

26 m
13 m

_____

4.

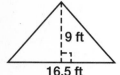
9 ft
16.5 ft

_____

5.

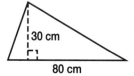
30 cm
80 cm

_____

6.

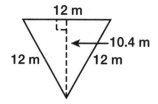
12 m
12 m
10.4 m
12 m

_____

Algebra • Expressions

Write an expression to represent the area of each triangle.

7.

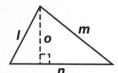
l
o
m
n

_____

8.

j
l
k

_____

9.

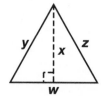
y
x
z
w

_____

Name _____   Date _____

Find the Circumference of a Circle

> The distance around a circle is called the **circumference**, or C.
> To find the approximate circumference, use the formula $C = \pi d$,
> where d is the diameter of the circle and π is the value 3.14 or $\frac{22}{7}$.
>
> $C = \pi d$
> $C = \pi \times 12 \text{ m}$
> $C = 37.68 \text{ m}$

Find the circumference of each circle. Use 3.14 for π.

1.

2 ft

_____

2.

100 miles

_____

3.

6 cm

_____

4.

8 m

_____

5.

1 in.

_____

6.

8 yd

_____

Express each circumference as a mixed number in simplest form.
Use $\frac{22}{7}$ for π.

7.

$\frac{1}{2}$ mile

_____

8.

$\frac{2}{3}$ m

_____

9.

$1\frac{1}{4}$ ft

_____

Name _____ Date _____

Solid Figures

The surface area of a rectangular prism or a cube can be determined by adding the surface areas of all of the faces of the figure.

Find the total surface area of this rectangular prism:

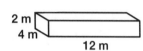

Face	Length	Width	Area
top	12 m	4 m	48 m^2
bottom	12 m	4 m	48 m^2
front	12 m	2 m	24 m^2
back	12 m	2 m	24 m^2
left side	4 m	2 m	8 m^2
right side	4 m	2 m	8 m^2
		sum:	160 m^2

Identify each figure. Then determine its surface area.

1.

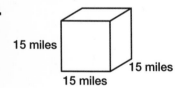

15 miles   15 miles   15 miles

2.

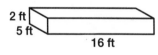

2 ft   5 ft   16 ft

3.

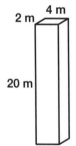

4 m   2 m   20 m

_____   _____   _____

Name _____ Date _____

Volume

The **volume** of a solid figure is a measure of the amount of space the figure occupies. Volume is measured in cubic units, or units^3.

Use $V = \ell \times w \times h$ to find the volume of a rectangular prism.

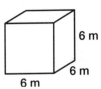

$V = \ell \times w \times h$

$V = 12 \text{ m} \times 3 \text{ m} \times 1 \text{ m}$

$V = 36 \text{ m}^3$

Use $V = s^3$ to find the volume of a cube.

$V = s^3$

$V = 6 \text{ m} \times 6 \text{ m} \times 6 \text{ m}$

$V = 216 \text{ m}^3$

Determine the volume of each solid figure.

1.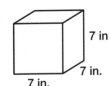

7 in

7 in.

7 in.

_____

2.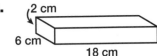

2 cm

6 cm

18 cm

_____

3.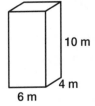

10 m

4 m

6 m

_____

Name _____   Date _____

Problem-Solving Application: Use Geometry

**Sometimes you can use what you know about geometry
to solve a problem.**

If a solid figure is made up of centimeter cubes, and you
are given three different two-dimensional views of the figure,
how could you build the figure?

- The top view shows you the number and
position of cubes in the bottom layer.

top

- The front view shows you that there are cubes
only in the right side of the top layer.

front

- The side view shows you that there are 3
layers of cubes in the back two rows.

right side

- Put the layers together to show a possible
answer.

Solve.

1. Sketch or build a three dimensional
figure with these views.

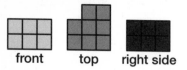

front   top   right side

Think: Which view tells you what must
be in the bottom layer to
support the other layers?

2. Sketch the front, top, and right-side
views of this solid figure.

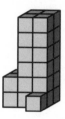

Think: How can you tell if there is a
small cube in place if it is
hidden from your view?

Name _____   Date _____

Meaning of Ratios

A box contains 7 balls and 5 cubes. How could you compare the number of cubes to the number of balls?

Step 1 Identify the terms of the ratio.

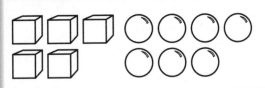

Step 2 Write the ratio.

The ratio of cubes to balls is 5 to 7.

The ratio 5 to 7 can also be written as 5:7 or $\frac{5}{7}$.

Write each ratio three different ways.

1. 25 girls to 15 boys

_____

2. 20 new cars to 60 old cars

_____

3. 13 apple-trees to 52 plum-trees

_____

4. 70 black reels to 14 white reels

_____

5. 8 cars to 32 tires

_____

6. 40 cookies to 15 people

_____

7. 24 pencils to 15 pens

_____

8. 12 cups to 10 saucers

_____

9. 7 forks to 12 spoons

_____

10. 14 chairs to 6 stools

_____

Name _____ Date _____

Equivalent Ratios

To make a pitcher of juice, 10 parts of water and 6 parts of concentrate are needed. If 20 parts of water are to be used, how many parts of concentrate are necessary?

Step 1 Write the ratio from the problem.

$$\frac{water}{} = \frac{10}{6}$$

Step 2 Write the ratio as a fraction in simplest form.

$$\frac{10}{6} = \frac{5}{3}$$

Step 3 Find a number to multiply by that gives 20 as the new first term.

$$\frac{5}{3} \times \frac{\blacksquare}{\blacksquare} = \frac{20}{\blacksquare}$$

Step 4 Find the unknown term. Multiply the numerator and denominator by 4.

$$\frac{5}{3} \times \frac{4}{4} = \frac{20}{12}$$

12 parts of concentrate are needed.

Write two equivalent ratios for each.

1. $\frac{3}{9}$

_____

2. $\frac{14}{22}$

_____

3. $\frac{12}{36}$

_____

4. $\frac{10}{35}$

_____

5. $\frac{10}{6}$

_____

6. $\frac{30}{25}$

_____

7. $\frac{18}{12}$

_____

8. $\frac{2}{15}$

_____

Name _____ Date _____

Rates

**In an all-day Run-Walk-a-thon, Ryan travels 21 kilometers in 3 hours.
At this rate, how many kilometers will he travel in 6 hours?**

Step 1 Find the rate in kilometers per hour. **Per** means *for each*.

$\frac{21}{3} = \frac{7}{1}$ = 7 kilometers per hour (kph)

Step 2 Multiply by the number of hours.

$7 \times 6 = 42$ kilometers.

Ryan will travel 42 kilometers in 6 hours.

Find the rate per unit of time.

1. 35 miles in 5 hours

_____

2. 40 meters in 10 seconds

_____

3. 200 miles in 20 days

_____

4. $100 for 10 hours

_____

5. $42 for 14 minutes

_____

6. $10,000 for 20 minutes

_____

7. 98 pages in 2 hours

_____

8. 65 blinks in 5 minutes

_____

9. 105 miles in 3 hours

_____

10. 17 inches in 1 minutes

_____

Name _____   Date _____

Scale Drawing

A scale is a ratio that compares measurements in a scale
drawing to measurements of real objects. You can use
equivalent ratios to find the height of the actual birdhouse.
The scale of the drawing is 1 inch:8 inches.

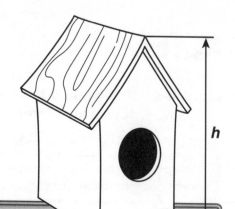

h

Step 1 Use an inch ruler to measure the height of the birdhouse in the drawing.

The birdhouse is 2 inches tall.

Step 2 Write the scale for the drawing in fraction form.

Each inch in the drawing represents 8 inches on the actual birdhouse, so the fraction is $\frac{1}{8}$.

Step 3 Write an equal ratio that shows the relationship between the height of the birdhouse in the drawing and its actual height.

$$\frac{1}{8} = \frac{2}{n}$$

Step 4 Find the height of the birdhouse.

$$\frac{1}{8} \times \frac{2}{2} = \frac{2}{16}$$

The actual birdhouse is 16 inches tall.

In a scale for a drawing of a home, 1 in. represents 2 ft.
The scale is 1 in.:2 ft. Find n in each case.

1. 5 in. represents n ft.

_____

2. 3 in. represents n ft.

_____

3. 10 in. represents n ft.

_____

4. n in. represents 4 ft.

_____

5. n in. represents 40 ft.

_____

6. n in. represents 100 ft.

_____

Name _____ Date _____

Problem-Solving Skill: Choose a Computation Method

To solve a problem you need to begin by making a plan.

Sometimes you can calculate mentally.
Tina is drawing a city map so that 1 in. represents 5 miles.
Her street, 8th Street, is 15 miles long. How long should the street
be on the map?

Think: Five miles are represented by one inch on the map,
so you need to divide each actual measure in miles by 5 to get the
number of inches for the drawing.

The length of 8th Street on the map will be 15 miles ÷ 5, or 3 in.

Sometimes you need to calculate on paper.
The Merced River is 225 km long. On a map with a scale of 1 cm:25 km,
how long should the Merced River be? Set up two equal ratios. The variable
n represents the unknown distance.

$\frac{1}{25} = \frac{n}{225}$

Think: What do I have to multiply 25 by to get 225?

$\frac{1 \times 9}{25 \times 9} = \frac{9}{255}$

$n = 9$, so the Merced River should be 9 cm long on the map.

---

1. A building is 150 m tall. A sketch of the building is done at scale of 1 inch:7.5 m. What should be the height of the building in the sketch ?

   Think: What equal ratios can I use to solve this problem?

2. On a city map, the distance between two subway stations is 6 in. The map has a scale of 1 inch:1,600 ft. What is the actual distance between the metro stations?

   Think: Can I solve this problem mentally?

Name _____ Date _____

Understand Percent

A percent is a ratio in which the second term is 100.

Step 1 On the grid paper, use a ruler to outline an area of 10 squares by 10 squares.

There are 100 small squares in the figure.

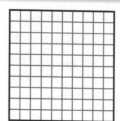

Step 2 Color 30 small squares red, 15 small squares blue, and 10 yellow.

What is the ratio of red squares to the total number of squares? 30 to 100.

What is the ratio of blue squares to the total number of squares? 15 to 100.

Step 3 Write each ratio as a percent.

The percent of red squares is 30%.
The percent of blue squares is 15%.
The percent of yellow squares is 10%.
The percent of colored squares is 55%.
The percent of uncolored squares is 45%.

Write the percent of each grid that is shaded.

1.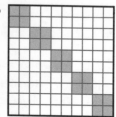

_____

2.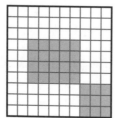

_____

3.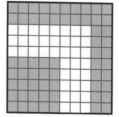

_____

Write each ratio as a percent.

4. $\frac{25}{100}$

_____

5. $\frac{13}{100}$

_____

6. $\frac{49}{100}$

_____

7. $\frac{82}{100}$

_____

Name _____ Date _____

Ratio and Percent

If 56% of students at Hadley High School learn French and $\frac{3}{10}$ learn German, what percent of these students learn German? What fraction of them learn French?

Write $\frac{3}{10}$ as a percent.

- Write an equivalent ratio with a denominator of 100.

$$\frac{3}{10} \times \frac{10}{10} = \frac{30}{100}$$

- Write the equivalent ratio using the percent symbol.

$$\frac{30}{100} = 30\%$$

Write 56% as a ratio in simplest form.

- Express the percent as an equivalent ratio.

$$56\% = \frac{56}{100}$$

- Try to find an equivalent ratio with the smallest possible first term.

$$\frac{56}{100} = \frac{28}{50} = \frac{14}{25}$$

30% of the students learn German and $\frac{14}{25}$ learn French.

Express each ratio as an equivalent percent and each percent as a ratio.

1. 86%

2. $\frac{17}{50}$

3. 72%

4. $\frac{12}{25}$

5. $\frac{3}{5}$

6. $\frac{11}{25}$

7. 33%

8. 92%

9. 50%

10. $\frac{3}{5}$

11. $\frac{9}{20}$

12. 55%

Name _____   Date _____

Decimals and Percents

Kelly scored 88% on her spelling test. You can also use
a decimal to express this score.

Express 88% in decimal form.

Step 1 Express the percent as a fraction.	**Step 2** Read the fraction in words. Then write it as a decimal.
$88\% = \frac{88}{100}$	$\frac{88}{100}$ means 88 hundredths. $\frac{88}{100} = 0.88$

Write each percent in decimal form and each decimal in percent form.

1. 73% _____

2. 0.02 _____

3. 0.6 _____

4. 52% _____

5. 6% _____

6. 22% _____

7. 0.56 _____

8. 39% _____

9. 0.68 _____

10. 48% _____

11. 0.56 _____

12. 0.91 _____

13. 0.78 _____

14. 0.5 _____

15. 28% _____

16. 0.88 _____

17. 0.9 _____

18. 39% _____

Name _____ Date _____

Use Fractions, Decimals, and Percents for Comparisons

Compare 42%, 0.65, and $\frac{1}{4}$.

Different Ways to Make Comparisons

You can use a number line to show parts of the whole.

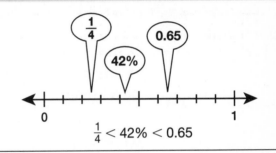

$\frac{1}{4} < 42\% < 0.65$

You can use equivalent decimals.

Step 1 To change the fraction to a decimal, divide the numerator by the denominator.	**Step 2** Think of the percent as a number of hundredths.	**Step 2** Compare 0.42, 0.65, and 0.25.
$\begin{array}{r} 0.25 \\ 4\overline{)1.00} \\ -8 \\ \hline 20 \\ -20 \\ \hline 0 \end{array}$	$42\% = 0.42$	$0.25 < 0.42 > 0.65$ So $\frac{1}{4} < 42\% < 0.65$

Which represents the greatest part of a unit?

1. 23% $\frac{9}{50}$ 0.25

   _____

2. $\frac{11}{20}$ 79%   0.5

   _____

3. 0.85   97% $\frac{23}{25}$

   _____

4. 30%   0.38 $\frac{1}{5}$

   _____

5. 0.16   57% $\frac{3}{4}$

   _____

6. 22% $\frac{1}{4}$ 0.28

   _____

7. $\frac{3}{20}$ 18%   0.2

   _____

8. $\frac{1}{5}$ 0.24   23%

   _____

Name _____   Date _____

Problem-Solving Strategy: Choose a Strategy

In a raffle drawing, each person has a 10% chance of winning.
How many people participated in the raffle?

Understand	**What is the question?** How many people participated in the raffle? **What do you know?** Each participant has a 10% chance of winning.
Plan	How can you solve this problem? You can draw a diagram or write an equation.
Solve	**Draw a Diagram** Outline 100 grid squares to represent 100%. Color 10 squares to represent the 10% chance. **Write an Equation** Set up equal ratios. $\frac{10}{100} = \frac{1}{n}$ Let n represent the total number of $\frac{10}{100} = \frac{1}{10}$ participants. 10 people participated in the raffle. $n = 10$
Look Back	Can you think of another way to solve the problem?

Solve. Choose the best strategy

1. Brenda scored 75% on her last geography test. On the next test, she got $\frac{23}{25}$ correct. On which test did she have a higher score?

> **Think:** How can I express 75% as a fraction and compare it to $\frac{23}{25}$?

_____

2. Heavy rains fell on 52% of the county one day and $\frac{12}{25}$ of the county the next day. On which day did a greater portion of the county receive heavy rain?

> **Think:** How can I express 52% as a fraction and compare it to $\frac{12}{25}$?

_____

3. Walt's favorite juice sells for $2.28 for a 32-oz bottle, or $4.25 for six 12-oz cans. Which one offers a better price?

> **Think:** Can I find the cost of one ounce?

_____

4. At the sporting goods store, tennis balls are sold in packages of 3 for $5.10 or 5 for $6.00. Which package offers the better price?

> **Think:** Can I find the cost of 15 balls?

_____

Name _____ Date _____

Mental Math: Find 10% of a Number

Cathy is delivering 30 meals to hospital patients. So far, she has delivered 10% of the meals. How many meals has she delivered?

Find 10% of 30.

Different Ways to Find 10% of a Number	
You can multiply by $\frac{1}{10}$. Finding 10% of a number is the same as finding $\frac{1}{10}$ of that number. $30 \times \frac{1}{10} = \frac{30}{1} \times \frac{1}{10} = \frac{30}{10} = 3$	**You can move the decimal point.** An easy way to find 10% of any number is to divide the number by 10 by moving the decimal point one place to the left. 10% of 30 = 3.0

Cathy has delivered 3 meals.

Find 10% of each number. Use mental math.

1. 84   **2.** 59   **3.** 9   **4.** 24

5. 359   **6.** 221   **7.** 3   **8.** 98

9. 929   **10.** 395   **11.** 32.9   **12.** 93.5

13. 5.10   **14.** 0.2   **15.** 0.08   **16.** 4.09

Name _____ Date _____

Percent of a Number

Find 75% of 640.

Different Ways to Find a Percent of a Number

You can write the percent as a fraction.

| **Step 1** Write the percent as a ratio. $75\% = \frac{75}{100} = \frac{3}{4}$ | **Step 2** Multiply. $\frac{3}{4} \times \frac{640}{1} = 480$ |

You can write the percent as a decimal.

| **Step 1** Write the percent as a decimal. $75\% = 75$ hundredths $= 0.75$ | **Step 2** Multiply. $\overset{2}{\underset{}{6}}\overset{2}{4}0$ 2 decimal places in the factors → $\times\ 0.75$ $\underline{32\ 00}$ $\underline{448\ 00}$ 2 decimal places in the product → 480.00 |

You can use equivalent ratios.

| **Step 1** Write the percent as a ratio in simplest form. $75\% = \frac{75}{100} = \frac{3}{4}$ | **Step 2** Write an equivalent ratio with the original number as the second term. $\frac{3}{4} = \frac{n}{640}$ $\frac{3}{4} \times \frac{160}{160} = \frac{480}{640}$ $n = 480$ |

Solve.

1. 20% of 50

2. 40% of 80

3. 80% of 25

_____

_____

_____

4. 65% of 30

5. 85% of 300

6. 50% of 36

_____

_____

_____

7. 45% of 90

8. 46% of 50

9. 38% of 82

_____

_____

_____

Name _____ Date _____

Compare Data Sets

Compare: 8 out of 40 ◯ 5 out of 20

Step 1 Write each fraction in simplest form. $\frac{8}{40} = \frac{1}{5}$ $\frac{5}{20} = \frac{1}{4}$	**Step 2** Express each fraction as a percent. $\frac{1}{5} = \frac{20}{100} = 20\%$ $\frac{1}{4} = \frac{25}{100} = 25\%$

So, 5 out of 20 > 8 out of 40.

**Write each set as a fraction in simplest form and as a percent.
Then order the percents from least to greatest.**

1. 3 out of 20; 5 out of 25; 6 out of 30

_____

_____

_____

_____

2. 20 out of 50; 16 out of 20; 18 out of 30

_____

_____

_____

_____

3. 42 out of 60; 36 out of 60; 81 out of 90

_____

_____

_____

_____

4. 13 out of 65; 84 out of 120; 75 out of 150

_____

_____

_____

_____

Name _____ Date _____

Problem-Solving Application: Use Percent

The graph shows the composition of a certain material. Carbon makes up 20% of the material. Find the measure of the central angle for the part of the circle graph that represents carbon's share of the total.

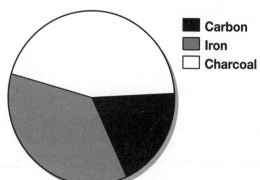

■ Carbon
■ Iron
□ Charcoal

Understand the question
What is the measure of the central angle for carbon's section of the circle graph?

Plan Multiply 360° by carbon's percent to find the number of degrees in its section.

Solve 20% × 360 = 0.20 × 360 = 72
The angle that represents carbon measures 72°.

Look Back Does 72° out of 360° seem about right to represent 20%?

Solve.

1. Calculate the angles for the other materials.
   Iron 35%
   Charcoal 45%
   Use a protractor to divide a circle into parts with the central angles you calculated. Label the parts.

   Think: What should be the sum of the three angles?

   _____

   _____

   _____

2. Another material is made up of the following substances:
   5 oz carbon
   15 oz charcoal
   20 oz iron
   10 oz ash
   Make a circle graph to show the percent of the total for each substance.

   Think: How many ounces are there in all?

   _____

   _____

   _____

Name _____   Date _____

Transformations

A transformation is a change in the position of a figure.

The movement of a figure along a straight line is called a translation.	The flip of a figure over a line is called a reflection.	The turn of a figure around a point is called a rotation.
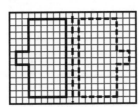	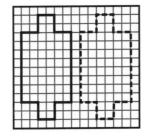	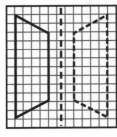

Tell whether the transformation is a translation, reflection, or rotation.

Example The figure has turned around a point, so this transformation is a rotation. 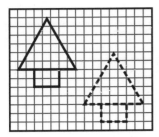	**1.** 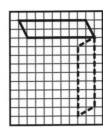 _____	**2.** 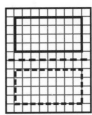 _____
3. 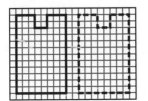 _____	**4.** _____	**5.** 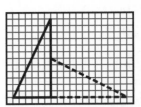 _____
6. 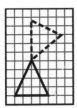 _____	**7.**  _____	**8.** _____

Name _____   Date _____

Integers and the Coordinate Plane

On a coordinate plane, the horizontal axis is called the
x-axis. The vertical axis is called the *y*-axis.

You can describe any
location on the grid
using an ordered pair.

  Point *P* is located at ($^-$3, $^+$4)

  To reach point *P* from the
  origin, you move left to
  $^-$3 and up to $^+$4.

  $^-$3 is called the
  x-coordinate of
  the point.

  $^+$4 is called the
  y-coordinate of
  the point.

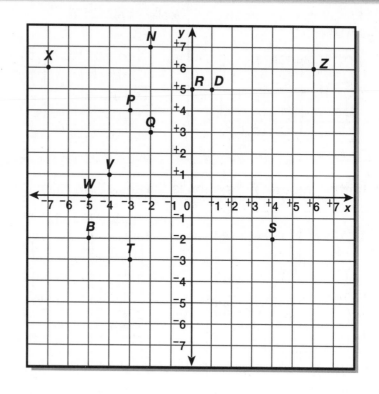

Write the ordered pair for each point or the letter name of the ordered pair.

1. R _____   **2.** T _____   **3.** S _____

4. B _____   **5.** V _____   **6.** W _____

7. ($^-$7, $^+$6) _____   **8.** (0, $^+$5) _____   **9.** ($^+$1, $^+$5) _____

10. ($^+$6, $^+$6) _____   **11.** ($^-$2, $^+$3) _____   **12.** ($^-$2, $^+$7) _____

Name _____ Date _____

Transformations in the Coordinate Plane

Describe the translation that would move a point at the origin to point C.

The movement of a point at the origin to point C can be described as two translations: $^+1$ followed by $^+4$.

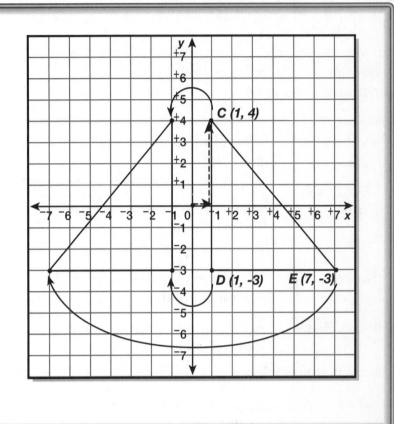

Describe each combination of translations.

1. from C to D _____

2. from E to C _____

3. from D to E _____

4. from D to the origin _____

5. from the origin to E _____

6. from E to D _____

7. from D to C _____

8. from C to E _____

Name _____ Date _____

Problem-Solving Strategy: Draw a Diagram

Sometimes you can solve a problem by drawing a diagram.
In how many different ways will a rhombus fit into a
congruent-size hole?

Understand	**What is the question?** In how many ways will the piece fit into the hole? **What do you know?** A rhombus has four congruent sides.
Plan	**How can you find the answer?** You can draw a rhombus and hole and see how many ways the rhombus fits over the hole.
Solve	The tracing fits four ways: two from rotating the rhombus and two from flipping the rhombus and rotating.
Look Back	Are there any other transformations of the rhombus that would make it fit exactly over the hole?

Draw a diagram to solve each problem.

1. How many ways will a regular pentagon–shaped piece fit into a congruent hole?

Think: Did I try flipping the pentagon and turning it to check all possibilities?

_____

2. How many ways will an isosceles triangle–shaped piece fit into a congruent hole?

Think: Did I try flipping the triangle and turning it to check all possibilities?

_____

3. How many different ways will a rectangular piece fit into a congruent hole?

Think: How is the problem similar to the others? How is it different?

4. How many ways will a regular octagon–shaped piece fit into a congruent hole?

Think: Did I try flipping the piece and turning it to check all possibilities?

_____

Name _____   Date _____

Integers and Functions

For the function $y = 6 - x$, find the value of y for each x
from ⁻2 to ⁺2.

Step 1 Make a function table to show values
of x and y from the function $y = 6 - x$.

$y = 6 - x$

x	y

Step 2 Write the integers from ⁻2 to ⁺2 in
the x-column. Then apply the function to each
x-value to get the resulting y-value.

$y = 6 - x$

x	y
⁻2	⁺8
⁻1	⁺7
0	⁺6
⁺1	⁺5
⁺2	⁺4

Complete each function table or find the function.

1. $y = 1 + x$

x	y
0	
⁺1	
⁺2	
⁺3	

2. $y = x - 5$

x	y
⁻3	
⁻2	
⁻1	
0	

3. $x - 1 = y$

x	y
⁺5	
⁺4	
⁺3	
0	

4. $y =$ _____

x	y
⁺5	⁺2
⁺6	⁺3
⁺7	⁺4
⁺10	⁺7

5. $y =$ _____

x	y
⁺1	⁺4
⁺0	⁺3
⁻1	⁺2
⁻4	⁻1

6. $y =$ _____

x	y
⁺6	⁺4
⁺7	⁺5
⁺8	⁺6
⁺3	⁺1

Name _____   Date _____

Problem-Solving Skill: Choose an Equation

Maria and her Mom planted bean plants. They measured the height of the plants each day. Which equation best describes the relationship between the day (*d*) and the height of the plant (*h*) in cm?

day	7	8	9
height	15	17	19

Equations: A: $h = d + 8$ **B:** $h = 5d - 10$ **C:** $h = 2d + 1$

Test each equation by substituting any ordered pair into each equation. Try (8,17).

A: $h = d + 8$
$17 = 8 + 8$
$17 \neq 16$

not true

B: $h = 5d - 10$
$17 = (5 \times 8) - 10$
$17 = 40 - 10$
$17 \neq 30$

not true

C: $h = 2d + 1$
$17 = (2 \times 8) + 1$
$17 = 16 + 1$
$17 = 17$

true

The equation that describes the relationship between (*d*) and (*h*) is $h = 2d + 1$.

Choose the equation that describes each situation.

1. The height of the plants (*h*) in Maria's garden increases as she gives the plants more gallons of water (*w*). What equation shows the relationship between height (*h*) and water (*w*)?

water	20	30	40	50
height	10	15	20	25

Think: Which equation describes the relationship between height (*h*) and water (*w*)?

a. $h = 3w$
b. $h = w \div 2$
c. $h = 2w + 3$

2. Maria and her Mother sold their vegetables at the farmer's market. They noticed that there was a relationship between the price (*p*) of the vegetables, and the number of vegetables sold (*s*).

price (in cents)	50¢	100¢	150¢
number sold	30	55	80

Think: Which equation describes the relationship between price (*p*) and number sold (*s*)?

a. $s = \frac{1}{2}p$

b. $s = \frac{1}{2}p + 5$

c. $p = s - 50$

Name _____   Date _____

Graph an Equation

Graph the equation $y = x - 3$ on a coordinate plane.

Step 1 Make a function table to find the ordered pairs. Use values for x from $^-3$ to $^+3$.

Rule:
$y = x - 3$

x	y
$^-3$	$^-6$
$^-2$	$^-5$
$^-1$	$^-4$
0	$^-3$
$^+1$	$^-2$
$^+2$	$^-1$
$^+3$	0

Step 2 Graph each ordered pair on a coordinate plane.

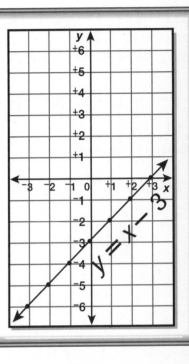

Find values of y to complete each table. Then graph the straight line equation.

1. $y = x + 4$

x	y
$^-2$	
$^-1$	
0	
$^+1$	
$^+2$	

2. $y = (2x) + 3$

x	y
$^-1$	
0	
$^+1$	
$^+2$	
$^+4$	

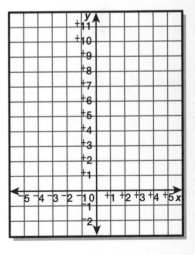

Name _____   Date _____

Problem-Solving Application: Use a Graph

The number of students who visit the library increases by 5 each week. If 25 students visited the library in the first week, how many will visit in the 8th week?

Understand	**What is the question?** How many students will visit the library in the 8th week? **What do you know?** 25 students visited in the first week. The number of students visiting increases by 5 each week.
Plan	**What can you do to find the answer?** Write ordered pairs in a function table. Look for a pattern, then write an equation to describe it. Then substitute 8 into the equation and solve.
Solve	Write the ordered pairs in a table. Let x represent the week, and y represent the number of students. The equation is $y = 5x + 20$. If $x = 8$, $y = (5 \times 8) + 20 = 60$. 60 students will visit the library in the 8th week.
Look Back	**Is your answer reasonable?**

Table (within Solve):

x	y
1	25
2	30
3	35
4	40

Use a function table and an equation to solve each problem.

1. 120 books were already checked out of the library. The number of books checked out from the library increases by 6 for every student who visits the library. How many would be checked out of the library after the fifth student visited the library?

Think: If you start with the number of students (x), what operation do you need to do to get (y), the number of books?

2. The library has 1,000 books. If they add 50 books per week to their collection, how many books will they have by week 5?

Think: If you start with the week (x), what operation do you need to do to get (y), the number of books?

_____

Name _____ Date _____

Read and Write Numbers

The value of a digit depends on its place in the number.

Number	Word Name	
<u>1</u>,365	one thousand, three hundred sixty-five	1 is in the thousands place and equals 1,000.
<u>4</u>2,790	forty-two thousand, seven hundred ninety	4 is in the ten thousands place and equals 40,000.

Write the number.

1. two thousand, five hundred twenty-three _____

2. thirty-six thousand, six hundred forty-one _____

3. nine thousand, four hundred ten _____

4. twenty-eight thousand, four hundred sixty-five _____

5. fifty thousand, seven hundred nineteen _____

Write the place and value of the underlined digit.

6. 4,5<u>9</u>2 _____   7. <u>8</u>,420 _____

8. 5,<u>3</u>60 _____   9. 21,78<u>2</u> _____

10. <u>4</u>7,106 _____   11. 73,<u>9</u>64 _____

12. <u>7</u>,539 _____   13. 92,<u>4</u>88 _____

14. 6,<u>5</u>20 _____   15. <u>8</u>3,026 _____

Name _____   Date _____

Write Numbers in Standard and Expanded Form

Use the value of a digit to write a number in expanded form.

Standard Form	Expanded Form
865	800 + 60 + 5
4,675	4,000 + 600 + 70 + 5
53,240	50,000 + 3,000 + 200 + 40

Write the number in standard form.

1. 4,000 + 200 + 60 + 1   _____

2. 30,000 + 1,000 + 400 + 90 + 2   _____

3. 60,000 + 4,000 + 200 + 70 + 3   _____

4. 10,000 + 4,000 + 300   _____

5. 7,000 + 300 + 80 + 4   _____

6. 8,000 + 200 + 70 + 5   _____

Write the number in expanded form.

7. 597   _____

8. 4,392   _____

9. 37,861   _____

10. 26,743   _____

11. 7,904   _____

12. 45,962   _____

Name _____ Date _____

Round 3- and 4-Digit Numbers

Round numbers to estimate about how many.

Round to the nearest:	Ten	Hundred	Thousand
19	20		
486	490	500	
4,623	4,620	4,600	5,000

Look at the number to the right of the number to be to be rounded.
If it is 5 or more, round up. If it is less than 5, round down.

Round to the nearest ten.

1. 461 _____ 2. 139 _____ 3. 575 _____

4. 782 _____ 5. 206 _____ 6. 827 _____

Round to the nearest hundred.

7. 238 _____ 8. 789 _____ 9. 323 _____

10. 410 _____ 11. 567 _____ 12. 836 _____

13. 3,721 _____ 14. 8,664 _____ 15. 6,133 _____

16. 9,484 _____ 17. 2,890 _____ 18. 1,111 _____

Round to the nearest thousand.

19. 7,354 _____ 20. 8,641 _____ 21. 5,814 _____

22. 6,407 _____ 23. 3,762 _____ 24. 9,185 _____

Name _____ Date _____

Round 5-Digit Numbers

Begin by finding the place you are rounding to.

Round to the nearest:	Thousand	Ten Thousand
36,676	37,000	40,000
43,244	43,000	40,000
67,821	68,000	70,000

Round to the nearest thousand.

1. 56,292 _____
2. 31,719 _____
3. 84,229 _____

4. 24,830 _____
5. 72,327 _____
6. 91,048 _____

7. 43,871 _____
8. 12,208 _____
9. 63,935 _____

10. 63,209 _____
11. 54,600 _____
12. 17,643 _____

Round to the nearest ten thousand.

13. 10,751 _____
14. 71,981 _____
15. 26,487 _____

16. 83,592 _____
17. 18,572 _____
18. 67,018 _____

19. 93,594 _____
20. 53,704 _____
21. 79,317 _____

22. 35,728 _____
23. 48,532 _____
24. 61,530 _____

Name _____ Date _____

Compare Numbers

To compare numbers, start at the left and compare digits in each place.

Compare

4,522 $>$ 4,361   Since 5 > 3, 4,522 > 4,361.

4,361 $<$ 4,522   Since 3 < 5, 4,361 < 4,522.

4,361 $=$ 4,361   Since all digits are equal, 4,361 = 4,361.

Compare. Write <, >, or = for each ◯.

1. 345 ◯ 452
2. 642 ◯ 872
3. 721 ◯ 721

4. 674 ◯ 643
5. 910 ◯ 901
6. 528 ◯ 542

7. 548 ◯ 542
8. 836 ◯ 836
9. 163 ◯ 168

10. 4,786 ◯ 8,900
11. 5,734 ◯ 3,901
12. 3,861 ◯ 4,861

13. 3,521 ◯ 3,521
14. 6,840 ◯ 6,954
15. 1,250 ◯ 1,520

16. 8,435 ◯ 8,436
17. 3,272 ◯ 3,271
18. 7,506 ◯ 7,500

19. 24,872 ◯ 34,872
20. 16,082 ◯ 61,082
21. 27,543 ◯ 17,543

22. 86,410 ◯ 86,410
23. 69,742 ◯ 69,732
24. 83,529 ◯ 83,526

Name _____   Date _____

Order Numbers

Begin ordering numbers by lining up the digits. Then start at
the left and compare digits in each place.

4,324 ← least		
4,578		
5,617 ← greatest		

| Greatest to least: | 5,617 | 4,578 | 4,324 |
| Least to greatest: | 4,324 | 4,578 | 5,617 |

Order from greatest to least.

1. 539   590   639   _____

2. 162   160   167   _____

3. 3,425   5,879   2,017   _____

4. 4,512   4,326   4,362   _____

5. 56,302   52,893   49,841   _____

6. 49,100   44,100   44,700   _____

Order from least to greatest.

7. 845   854   450   _____

8. 973   970   954   _____

9. 5,672   5,384   5,734   _____

10. 8,349   7,349   8,439   _____

11. 32,640   32,496   39,532   _____

12. 78,615   87,615   78,415   _____

Name _____ Date _____

Addition: Regrouping Ones

Add. Regroup if necessary.

Step 1 Add the ones. Regroup 16 ones as 1 ten 6 ones.

Step 2 Add the tens and hundreds.

$$\begin{array}{r} \overset{1}{3}59 \\ +\ 117 \\ \hline 476 \end{array}$$

Step 1 Add the ones.

Step 2 Add the tens. Regroup 11 tens as 1 hundred 1 ten.

Step 3 Add the hundreds and the thousands.

$$\begin{array}{r} 4,\overset{1}{5}24 \\ +\ 2,395 \\ \hline 6,919 \end{array}$$

Add.

1. 462 + 315
2. 217 + 238
3. 538 + 191
4. 626 + 283

5. 345 + 416
6. 727 + 248
7. 426 + 492
8. 345 + 416

9. 3,216 + 1,447
10. 4,296 + 3,133
11. 5,183 + 2,744
12. 2,754 + 6,532

13. 5,483 + 2,382
14. 8,126 + 1,308
15. 4,218 + 3,557
16. 6,433 + 4,381

17. 5,224 + 3,117
18. 3,884 + 2,915
19. 6,437 + 3,722
20. 4,395 + 4,554

Name _____   Date _____

Addition: Regrouping Twice

Sometimes you need to regroup twice.

Step 1 Add the ones. Regroup 16 ones as 1 ten 6 ones.	**Step 1** Add the ones. Regroup 10 ones as 1 ten 0 ones.
Step 2 Add the tens. Regroup 15 tens as 1 hundred 5 tens.	**Step 2** Add the tens. Regroup 19 tens as 1 hundred 9 tens.
Step 3 Add the hundreds.	**Step 3** Add the hundreds and thousands.

$$\begin{array}{r} {\scriptstyle 11} \\ 2\mathbf{69} \\ +\ 187 \\ \hline 456 \end{array}$$

$$\begin{array}{r} {\scriptstyle 11} \\ 3,4\mathbf{95} \\ +\ 2,\mathbf{395} \\ \hline 5,890 \end{array}$$

Add.

1. $\begin{array}{r} 376 \\ +\ 285 \\ \hline \end{array}$

2. $\begin{array}{r} 294 \\ +\ 488 \\ \hline \end{array}$

3. $\begin{array}{r} 729 \\ +\ 196 \\ \hline \end{array}$

4. $\begin{array}{r} 648 \\ +\ 286 \\ \hline \end{array}$

5. $\begin{array}{r} 427 \\ +\ 396 \\ \hline \end{array}$

6. $\begin{array}{r} 538 \\ +\ 195 \\ \hline \end{array}$

7. $\begin{array}{r} 863 \\ +\ 178 \\ \hline \end{array}$

8. $\begin{array}{r} 195 \\ +\ 118 \\ \hline \end{array}$

9. $\begin{array}{r} 3,418 \\ +\ 2,717 \\ \hline \end{array}$

10. $\begin{array}{r} 4,523 \\ +\ 1,684 \\ \hline \end{array}$

11. $\begin{array}{r} 7,436 \\ +\ 2,993 \\ \hline \end{array}$

12. $\begin{array}{r} 3,452 \\ +\ 4,871 \\ \hline \end{array}$

13. $\begin{array}{r} 5,620 \\ +\ 1,389 \\ \hline \end{array}$

14. $\begin{array}{r} 4,038 \\ +\ 2,886 \\ \hline \end{array}$

15. $\begin{array}{r} 5,384 \\ +\ 3,496 \\ \hline \end{array}$

16. $\begin{array}{r} 7,266 \\ +\ 1,971 \\ \hline \end{array}$

17. $\begin{array}{r} 4,527 \\ +\ 2,891 \\ \hline \end{array}$

18. $\begin{array}{r} 3,994 \\ +\ 1,872 \\ \hline \end{array}$

19. $\begin{array}{r} 7,218 \\ +\ 2,834 \\ \hline \end{array}$

20. $\begin{array}{r} 5,185 \\ +\ 4,377 \\ \hline \end{array}$

Name _____ Date _____

Subtraction: Regrouping Once

Begin by subtracting the ones. Regroup if necessary.

Step 1 Regroup 1 ten as 10 ones to make 18 ones. Subtract the ones. **Step 2** Subtract the tens and hundreds.	**Step 1** Subtract the ones. **Step 2** Regroup 1 hundred as 10 tens. Subtract the tens, hundreds, and thousands.

$$
\begin{array}{r} \overset{5\ 18}{4\cancel{68}} \\ -149 \\ \hline 319 \end{array}
\qquad
\begin{array}{r} \overset{8\ 10}{3,9\cancel{0}7} \\ -1,317 \\ \hline 2,590 \end{array}
$$

Subtract.

1. $\begin{array}{r} 547 \\ -\ 228 \\ \hline \end{array}$ **2.** $\begin{array}{r} 697 \\ -\ 182 \\ \hline \end{array}$ **3.** $\begin{array}{r} 473 \\ -\ 317 \\ \hline \end{array}$ **4.** $\begin{array}{r} 823 \\ -\ 308 \\ \hline \end{array}$

5. $\begin{array}{r} 724 \\ -\ 243 \\ \hline \end{array}$ **6.** $\begin{array}{r} 935 \\ -\ 518 \\ \hline \end{array}$ **7.** $\begin{array}{r} 638 \\ -\ 362 \\ \hline \end{array}$ **8.** $\begin{array}{r} 853 \\ -\ 472 \\ \hline \end{array}$

9. $\begin{array}{r} 4,398 \\ -\ 1,279 \\ \hline \end{array}$ **10.** $\begin{array}{r} 5,288 \\ -\ 3,269 \\ \hline \end{array}$ **11.** $\begin{array}{r} 6,821 \\ -\ 3,618 \\ \hline \end{array}$ **12.** $\begin{array}{r} 6,499 \\ -\ 2,115 \\ \hline \end{array}$

13. $\begin{array}{r} 8,532 \\ -\ 5,127 \\ \hline \end{array}$ **14.** $\begin{array}{r} 9,824 \\ -\ 4,317 \\ \hline \end{array}$ **15.** $\begin{array}{r} 7,136 \\ -\ 3,128 \\ \hline \end{array}$ **16.** $\begin{array}{r} 6,824 \\ -\ 5,281 \\ \hline \end{array}$

17. $\begin{array}{r} 8,487 \\ -\ 6,318 \\ \hline \end{array}$ **18.** $\begin{array}{r} 7,532 \\ -\ 5,327 \\ \hline \end{array}$ **19.** $\begin{array}{r} 6,492 \\ -\ 5,327 \\ \hline \end{array}$ **20.** $\begin{array}{r} 8,487 \\ -\ 6,318 \\ \hline \end{array}$

Name _____   Date _____

Subtraction: Regrouping Twice

Sometimes you need to regroup twice.

Step 1 Regroup 1 ten as 10 ones to make 17 ones. Subtract the ones. **Step 2** Regroup 1 hundred to make 12 tens. Subtract the tens and hundreds.	$\begin{array}{r} \overset{12}{3\,\overset{2}{\cancel{4}}\,\overset{17}{\cancel{3}}\cancel{7}} \\ -\,2\,8\,8 \\ \hline 1\,4\,9 \end{array}$
Step 1 Regroup 1 ten as 10 ones to make 12 ones. Subtract the ones. **Step 2** Regroup 1 hundred to make 11 tens. Subtract the tens, hundreds, and thousands.	$\begin{array}{r} \overset{8}{3},\overset{11}{\cancel{9}}\,\overset{1}{\cancel{2}}\,\overset{12}{\cancel{2}} \\ -\,1,3\,7\,7 \\ \hline 2,5\,4\,5 \end{array}$

Subtract.

1.	538 − 279	**2.**	624 − 376	**3.**	945 − 487	**4.**	721 − 183

5.	872 − 484	**6.**	463 − 285	**7.**	726 − 547	**8.**	548 − 279

9.	4,672 − 3,728	**10.**	3,189 − 1,890	**11.**	7,394 − 2,845	**12.**	8,922 − 7,465

13.	8,322 − 6,441	**14.**	9,624 − 4,940	**15.**	7,346 − 3,158	**16.**	4,179 − 2,994

17.	6,418 − 3,379	**18.**	8,748 − 3,956	**19.**	3,211 − 1,156	**20.**	5,397 − 2,409

Name _____   Date _____

Subtraction: Across Zeros

Regroup several times.

Step 1 Regroup 1 ten as 10 ones to make 16 ones. Subtract the ones.	**Step 1** Regroup 1 thousand as 10 hundreds. Regroup 1 hundred as 10 tens. Regroup 1 ten as 10 ones to make 17 ones.
Step 2 Subtract the tens. Regroup 1 thousand to make 10 hundreds. Subtract the hundreds.	3 10 2 16 $~~~~$ 4̸0̸3̸6̸ $~~$ − 1 4 2 8 $~~~~~$ 2,6 0 8
Step 3 Subtract the thousands.	

Right box:
9 9
4 10 10 17
5̸0̸0̸7̸
− 2,3 0 8
2,6 9 9

Step 2 Subtract the ones, tens, hundreds, and thousands.

Subtract.

1. 407 − 324
2. 850 − 662
3. 180 − 130
4. 603 − 291

5. 801 − 123
6. 500 − 304
7. 607 − 200
8. 904 − 526

9. 4,302 − 2,236
10. 6,200 − 3,800
11. 7,041 − 1,642
12. 8,507 − 4,515

13. 8,004 − 3,721
14. 9,402 − 5,196
15. 8,500 − 2,307
16. 3,004 − 1,208

17. 5,094 − 3,120
18. 7,670 − 4,589
19. 8,210 − 5,131
20. 9,704 − 6,608

Name _____   Date _____

Estimate Sums and Differences

Estimate by rounding to the greatest place.

469	rounds to	500		6,789	rounds to	7,000
+ 221	rounds to	+ 200		+ 3,351	rounds to	+ 3,000
		700				4,000

Estimate by rounding to the greatest place.

1.   549
        + 236   + _____

2.   610
        + 332   + _____

3.   275
        + 298   + _____

4.   478
        + 165   + _____

5.   5,398
        + 1,824   + _____

6.   7,042
        + 2,165   + _____

7.   3,425
        + 4,768   + _____

8.   5,301
        + 4,322   + _____

9.   534
        + 209   + _____

10.   644
        − 487   − _____

11.   782
        − 580   − _____

12.   866
        − 539   − _____

13.   5,462
        − 3,284   − _____

14.   8,720
        − 4,962   − _____

15.   9,010
        − 7,665   − _____

Name _____ Date _____

Add and Subtract Money

Write the dollar sign and decimal point when adding
and subtracting money.

> **Start at the right. Add or subtract the hundredths and tenths. Write the decimal point.**
> **Add or subtract the ones and tens. Be sure to write the dollar sign.**
>
> $4.31 $54.35
> + 2.83   − 13.55
> $7.14 $40.80

Add.

1. $4.39
   + 2.14

2. $3.50
   + 4.86

3. $7.25
   + 3.18

4. $5.27
   + 1.68

5. $15.50
   + 23.96

6. $19.95
   + 39.90

7. $52.40
   + 17.80

8. $63.45
   + 14.90

Subtract.

9. $5.95
   − 3.60

10. $4.90
   − 3.05

11. $8.00
   − 2.25

12. $9.95
   − 6.39

13. $15.50
   − 13.00

14. $63.75
   − 14.50

15. $83.29
   − 37.10

16. $95.00
   − 15.95

Name _____   Date _____

Use Properties of Addition

Addition properties can help you add.

Commutative Property:	$34 + 25 = 25 + 34$
Associative Property:	$3 + (2 + 5) = (3 + 2) + 5$
Identity Property:	$0 + 45 = 45$

Add. Write the name of the property that helps.

1. $16 + 18 =$ _____ $18 + 16 =$ _____   _____

2. $0 + 379 =$ _____   _____

3. $6 + (9 + 4) =$ _____   _____

4. $31 + 0 =$ _____   _____

5. $420 + 125 =$ _____ $125 + 420 =$ _____   _____

6. $841 + 0 =$ _____   _____

7. $(14 + 18) + 10 =$ _____   _____

8. $50 + 40 =$ _____ $40 + 50 =$ _____   _____

9. $0 + 598 =$ _____   _____

10. $12 + 13 =$ _____ $13 + 12 =$ _____   _____

11. $98 + 0 =$ _____   _____

12. $(20 + 25) + 5 =$ _____   _____

13. $246 + 125 =$ _____ $125 + 246 =$ _____   _____

Name _____   Date _____

Use Properties of Multiplication

Multiplication properties can help you multiply.

Commutative Property:	$3 \times 2 = 2 \times 3$
Associative Property:	$4 \times (3 \times 2) = (4 \times 3) \times 2$
Identity Property:	$7 \times 0 = 0$ $7 \times 1 = 7$

Multiply. Write the name of the property that helps.

1. $6 \times 2 =$ _____ $2 \times 6 =$ _____   _____

2. $5 \times 1 =$ _____   _____

3. $5 \times (2 \times 3) =$ _____   _____

4. $9 \times 1 =$ _____   _____

5. $8 \times 3 =$ _____ $3 \times 8 =$ _____   _____

6. $1 \times 3 =$ _____   _____

7. $9 \times 8 =$ _____ $8 \times 9 =$ _____   _____

8. $(2 \times 4) \times 3 =$ _____   _____

9. $8 \times 7 =$ _____ $7 \times 8 =$ _____   _____

10. $4 \times 0 =$ _____   _____

11. $6 \times 1 =$ _____   _____

12. $7 \times 3 =$ _____ $3 \times 7 =$ _____   _____

13. $(5 \times 2) \times 1 =$ _____   _____

Name _____ Date _____

Find Factors

Factors of a number are the numbers that can be multiplied to give that number.

The **factors** of 4 are 1, 2, and 4.

$1 \times 4 = 4$

$4 \times 1 = 4$

$2 \times 2 = 4$

Write the factors for each number.

1. 3 _____

2. 6 _____

3. 7 _____

4. 5 _____

5. 9 _____

6. 8 _____

7. 12 _____

8. 18 _____

9. 21 _____

10. 10 _____

11. 36 _____

12. 32 _____

13. 27 _____

Name _____ Date _____

Find Multiples

Multiples of a number are the products of that number and other numbers.

> **Multiples** of 2 are 0, 2, 4, 6, 8, 10, 14, 16, 18, . . .
>
> **Multiples** of 6 are 0, 6, 12, 18, 24, 30, 36, 42, 48, 54, . . .
>
> **Multiples** of 10 are 0, 10, 20, 30, 40, 50, 60, 70, 80, . . .

Skip count and find the next 6 multiples.

1. Multiples of 3   0, 3, 6

   _____

2. Multiples of 5   0, 5, 10

   _____

3. Multiples of 8   0, 8, 16

   _____

4. Multiples of 4   0, 4, 8

   _____

5. Multiples of 7   0, 7, 14

   _____

6. Multiples of 9   0, 9, 18

   _____

Name _____   Date _____

Multiply by 1-Digit Numbers

Multiply. Regroup if necessary.

Step 1 Multiply the ones. Regroup as 2 tens 1 one.	**Step 1** Multiply the ones.
Step 2 Multiply the tens. 3×2 tens = 6 tens. Then add the regrouped tens to make 8 tens.	**Step 2** Multiply the tens. Regroup as 2 hundreds 1 ten.
	Step 3 Multiply the hundreds. 3×2 hundreds = 6 hundreds. Then add the regrouped hundreds to make 8 hundreds.

$$\begin{array}{r} \overset{2}{2}7 \\ \times\ 3 \\ \hline 81 \end{array}$$

$$\begin{array}{r} \overset{2}{2}73 \\ \times\ \ 3 \\ \hline 819 \end{array}$$

Multiply.

1.
$$\begin{array}{r} 19 \\ \times\ 3 \\ \hline \end{array}$$

2.
$$\begin{array}{r} 24 \\ \times\ 4 \\ \hline \end{array}$$

3.
$$\begin{array}{r} 14 \\ \times\ 3 \\ \hline \end{array}$$

4.
$$\begin{array}{r} 28 \\ \times\ 2 \\ \hline \end{array}$$

5.
$$\begin{array}{r} 18 \\ \times\ 3 \\ \hline \end{array}$$

6.
$$\begin{array}{r} 15 \\ \times\ 5 \\ \hline \end{array}$$

7.
$$\begin{array}{r} 12 \\ \times\ 7 \\ \hline \end{array}$$

8.
$$\begin{array}{r} 27 \\ \times\ 3 \\ \hline \end{array}$$

9.
$$\begin{array}{r} 39 \\ \times\ 3 \\ \hline \end{array}$$

10.
$$\begin{array}{r} 14 \\ \times\ 6 \\ \hline \end{array}$$

11.
$$\begin{array}{r} 13 \\ \times\ 4 \\ \hline \end{array}$$

12.
$$\begin{array}{r} 55 \\ \times\ 5 \\ \hline \end{array}$$

13.
$$\begin{array}{r} 218 \\ \times\ \ 4 \\ \hline \end{array}$$

14.
$$\begin{array}{r} 235 \\ \times\ \ 2 \\ \hline \end{array}$$

15.
$$\begin{array}{r} 443 \\ \times\ \ 2 \\ \hline \end{array}$$

16.
$$\begin{array}{r} 172 \\ \times\ \ 5 \\ \hline \end{array}$$

17.
$$\begin{array}{r} 313 \\ \times\ \ 4 \\ \hline \end{array}$$

18.
$$\begin{array}{r} 112 \\ \times\ \ 6 \\ \hline \end{array}$$

19.
$$\begin{array}{r} 323 \\ \times\ \ 8 \\ \hline \end{array}$$

20.
$$\begin{array}{r} 539 \\ \times\ \ 3 \\ \hline \end{array}$$

Name _____   Date _____

Estimate Products

Estimate by rounding to the greatest place.

374	400		5,129	5,000
× 2	× 2		× 4	× 4
	about 800			about 2,000

Estimate by rounding. Then multiply.

1. 824
        × 3   × _____

2. 789
        × 5   × _____

3. 170
        × 6   × _____

4. 508
        × 4   × _____

5. 636
        × 2   × _____

6. 215
        × 8   × _____

7. 366
        × 7   × _____

8. 945
        × 2   × _____

9. 712
        × 4   × _____

10. 293
         × 6   × _____

11. 438
         × 5   × _____

12. 430
         × 8   × _____

13. 5,420
         × 4   × _____

14. 3,901
         × 6   × _____

15. 8,645
         × 2   × _____

16. 4,321
         × 4   × _____

17. 7,854
         × 3   × _____

18. 7,854
         × 3   × _____

Name _____ Date _____

Multiply by 2-Digit Numbers

The value of a digit depends on its place in the number.

Step 1 Multiply by the ones place. 3 times 42. Write the numbers.	**Step 1** Multiply by the ones place. 3 times 35. Regroup as necessary. Write the numbers.
Step 2 Write a 0 in the ones place. Multiply by the tens. 1 times 42. Write the numbers.	**Step 2** Write a 0 in the ones place. Multiply by the tens. 2 times 35. Regroup as necessary. Write the numbers.
Step 3 Add.	**Step 3** Add.

Step column 1:
```
   42
 × 13
  126
+ 420
  546
```

Step column 2:
```
   1
  35
 × 23
  105
+ 700
  805
```

Multiply.

1. 15 × 25
2. 21 × 33
3. 36 × 18
4. 45 × 22

5. 29 × 32
6. 42 × 13
7. 28 × 21
8. 37 × 14

9. 66 × 11
10. 38 × 14
11. 53 × 23
12. 42 × 12

13. 16 × 15
14. 49 × 24
15. 51 × 17
16. 32 × 21

Name _____ Date _____

Divide by 1-Digit Numbers

Divide the numbers. Write the remainder.

Step 1 Divide 6 tens by 2.
Write the number.

Step 2 Divide 2 ones by 2.
Write the number.

$$\frac{31}{2\overline{)62}}$$

Step 1 Divide 5 tens by 3.
There are 2 tens left over.

Step 2 Regroup the 2 tens as 20 ones.
Add the 3 ones to make 23 ones.

Step 3 Divide 23 ones by 3.
There are 2 ones left over.

Step 4 Write the remainder.

$$\begin{array}{r} 17\ R2 \\ 3\overline{)53} \\ -3\downarrow \\ \hline 23 \\ -21 \\ \hline 2 \end{array}$$

Divide.

1. $3\overline{)27}$ **2.** $2\overline{)22}$ **3.** $4\overline{)19}$ **4.** $8\overline{)40}$

5. $5\overline{)51}$ **6.** $6\overline{)42}$ **7.** $3\overline{)57}$ **8.** $4\overline{)\,9}$

9. $5\overline{)68}$ **10.** $4\overline{)72}$ **11.** $8\overline{)84}$ **12.** $6\overline{)77}$

13. $4\overline{)56}$ **14.** $7\overline{)92}$ **15.** $3\overline{)63}$ **16.** $4\overline{)36}$

Name _____ Date _____

Measure to the Nearest Half Inch and Quarter Inch

Use an inch ruler to measure.

- - - - - - - - - - - - - - - - $2\frac{1}{4}$ inches

-                    3 inches

-    $4\frac{1}{4}$ inches

Use an inch ruler. Measure to the nearest inch, half inch, or quarter inch.

1. _____

2. _____

3. _____

4. _____

5. _____

6. _____

7. _____

8. _____

Name _____ Date _____

Measure to the Nearest Centimeter

Use a centimeter ruler to measure.

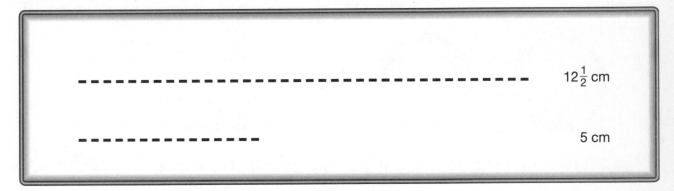

$12\frac{1}{2}$ cm

5 cm

Use a centimeter ruler. Measure to the nearest centimeter or half centimeter.

1. _____

2. _____

3. _____

4. _____

5. _____

6. _____

7. _____

8. _____

Name _____ Date _____

Elapsed Time to the Half-Hour

To find elapsed time, first count the hours. Then count the minutes.

$2\frac{1}{2}$ hours have passed.

The time is 3:30.

What time will it be?

1.  The meeting lasts for 30 minutes. _____

2. The bus ride lasts for 2 hours. _____

3. The trip lasts for $2\frac{1}{2}$ hours. _____

4. Lunch lasts for 1 hour. _____

5.  The movie lasts for 2 hours. _____

6. The party lasts for $1\frac{1}{2}$ hours. _____

Name _____ Date _____

Elapsed Time to 5 Minutes

To find elapsed time, first count the hours. Then count the minutes.

1 hour 20 minutes have passed.

The time is 4:20.

What time will it be?

1.   in 2 hours 15 minutes _____

2. **7:00** in 1 hour 10 minutes _____

3.   in 25 minutes _____

4.  in 1 hour 5 minutes _____

5.  **10:30** in 2 hours 35 minutes _____

6.   in 1 hour _____

Name _____   Date _____

Read a Thermometer in Degrees Fahrenheit

Use a Fahrenheit thermometer to measure the temperature.

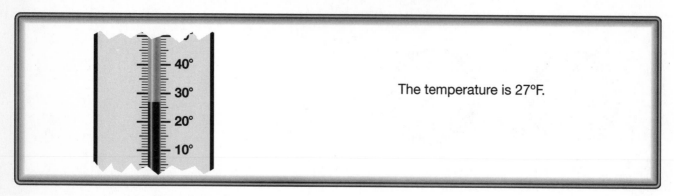

The temperature is 27°F.

Write the temperature in degrees Fahrenheit.

1.

70°
60°
50°
40°

_____

2.

10°
0°
⁻10°
⁻20°

_____

3.

90°
80°
70°
60°

_____

4.

120°
110°
100°
90°

_____

5.

10°
0°
⁻10°
⁻20°

_____

6.

120°
110°
100°
90°

_____

Name _____ Date _____

Read a Thermometer in Degrees Celsius

Use a Celsius thermometer to measure the temperature.

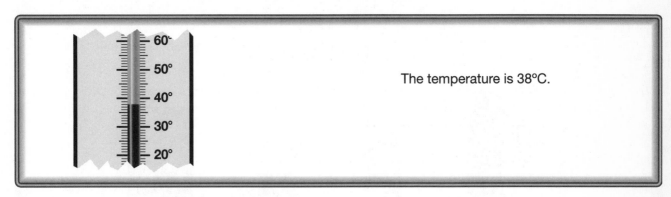

The temperature is 38°C.

Write the temperature in degrees Celsius.

1.

_____

2.

_____

3.

_____

4.

_____

5.

_____

6.

_____

Name _____ Date _____

Read and Interpret a Bar Graph

A bar graph shows information.

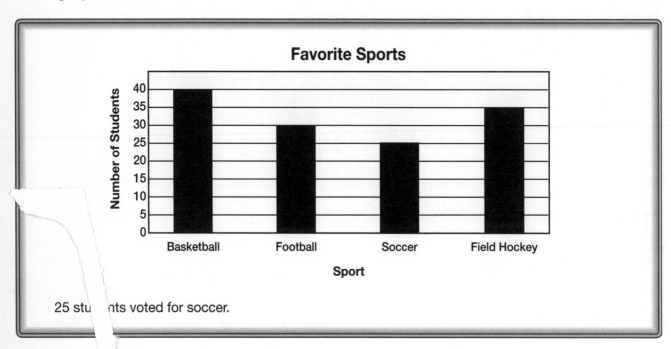

Favorite Sports

25 students voted for soccer.

Use the graph to answer the questions.

1. How many students voted for football? _____

2. Did more students vote for field hockey or basketball? _____

3. How many students voted for basketball? _____

4. How many students voted for field hockey and football? _____

5. Which sport got the greatest number of votes? _____

6. Which sport got the least number of votes? _____

7. If five more students voted for field hockey, how would you change the graph?

Name _____   Date _____

Read and Interpret a Line Graph

A line graph shows how information changes over time.

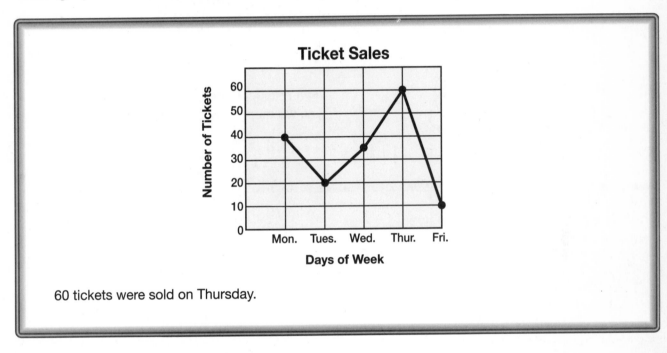

60 tickets were sold on Thursday.

Use the graph to answer the questions.

1. How many tickets were sold on Monday?   _____

2. Were more tickets sold on Tuesday or Wednesday?   _____

3. How many tickets were sold on Monday, Tuesday, and Wednesday?   _____

4. On which day were 35 tickets sold?   _____

5. On which day were the greatest number of tickets sold?   _____

6. On which day were the least number of tickets sold?   _____

7. If ten more tickets were sold on Friday,
   how would you change the graph?

   _____

Name _____ Date _____

Likelihood of an Event

Use the information to decide whether an event is likely to happen.

If you close your eyes and choose a fruit, you will most likely choose an orange.

Choose the most reasonable answer.

1. Maria wants to spin a 1.	certain	likely
2. Alex wants to spin a 4.	likely	impossible
3. Jane wants to spin a 3.	unlikely	likely
4. Jon wants to spin a 2.	certain	unlikely

5. Robert reaches in the bag. He wants to choose a circle.		impossible
6. Kate wants to choose a triangle.	...kely	unlikely
7. Anne wants to choose a square.	certain	unlikely
8. Dave wants to choose a circle.	likely	impossible

Name _____   Date _____

Write Fractions

A fraction names the equal parts of an object or a set.

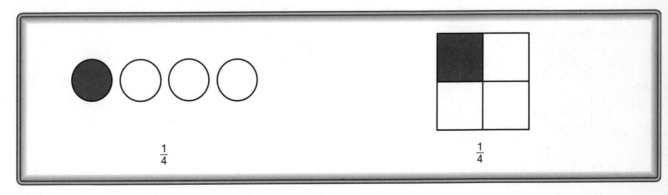

$\frac{1}{4}$ $\frac{1}{4}$

What part is shaded? Write the fraction.

1.

_____

2.

_____

3.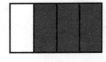

_____

4.

_____

5.

_____

6.

_____

What fraction names the point?

7.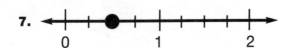

_____

8.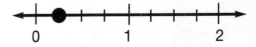

_____

Name _____   Date _____

Identify Equivalent Fractions

Equivalent fractions name the same part.

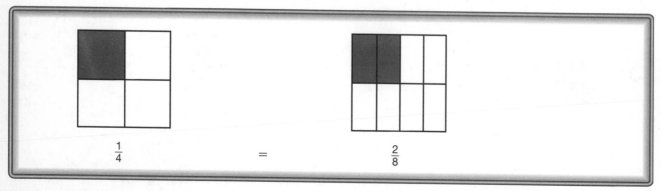

$$\frac{1}{4} \qquad = \qquad \frac{2}{8}$$

Write the equivalent fraction.

1.

$$\frac{1}{3} = \text{_____}$$

2.

$$\frac{5}{6} = \text{_____}$$

3.

$$\frac{2}{3} = \text{_____}$$

4.

$$\frac{3}{4} = \text{_____}$$

5.

$$\frac{3}{5} = \text{_____}$$

6.

$$\frac{3}{4} = \text{_____}$$

Name _____ Date _____

Compare Unit Fractions

Use >, <, and = to compare fractions.

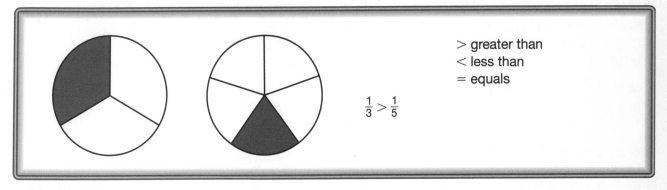

> greater than
< less than
= equals

$\frac{1}{3} > \frac{1}{5}$

Compare. Write >, <, or = for each ◯.

1.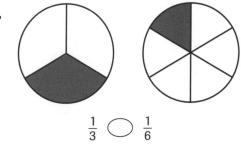

$\frac{1}{3}$ ◯ $\frac{1}{6}$

2.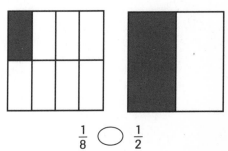

$\frac{1}{8}$ ◯ $\frac{1}{2}$

3. $\frac{1}{6}$ ◯ $\frac{1}{4}$

4. $\frac{1}{2}$ ◯ $\frac{1}{3}$

5. $\frac{1}{2}$ ◯ $\frac{1}{4}$

6. $\frac{1}{8}$ ◯ $\frac{1}{8}$

7. $\frac{1}{6}$ ◯ $\frac{1}{3}$

8. $\frac{1}{4}$ ◯ $\frac{1}{3}$

Name _____ Date _____

Multiply Money

Use the dollar sign and decimal point when you multiply money amounts.

Step 1 Multiply the hundredths. Regroup as 1 tenth 6 hundredths.

Step 2 Multiply the tenths. 2 × 2 tenths = 4 tenths. Then add the 1 regrouped tenth. 4 + 1 = 5

Step 3 Multiply the ones. 2 × 3 ones = 6 ones.

$$\begin{array}{r} \overset{1}{\$3.28} \\ \times\quad 2 \\ \hline \$6.56 \end{array}$$

Step 1 Multiply the hundredths. Regroup as 3 tenths 5 hundredths.

Step 2 Multiply the tenths. 5 × 2 tenths = 10 tenths. Then add the 3 regrouped tenths. 10 + 3 = 13. Regroup as 1 one and 3 tenths.

Step 3 Multiply the ones. 5 × 8 ones = 40 ones. 40 + 1 = 41

$$\begin{array}{r} \overset{1\,3}{\$8.27} \\ \times\quad 5 \\ \hline \$41.35 \end{array}$$

Multiply.

1. $1.24 × 3
2. $5.14 × 7
3. $1.25 × 4
4. $3.35 × 2

5. $6.13 × 8
6. $2.80 × 3
7. $3.98 × 9
8. $5.43 × 5

9. $3.22 × 6
10. $4.95 × 4
11. $1.79 × 5
12. $3.21 × 9

13. $4.60 × 4
14. $6.25 × 3
15. $2.75 × 5
16. $3.35 × 6

17. $2.43 × 7
18. $7.30 × 2
19. $1.11 × 8
20. $6.21 × 3

Name _____ Date _____

Divide Money

Use the dollar sign and decimal point when you divide money amounts.

Step 1 Divide 13 by 4. There is 1 left over.	$\begin{array}{r} \$3.25 \\ 4\overline{)\$13.00} \\ -12 \\ \hline 1\,0 \\ -\ 8 \\ \hline 20 \\ -20 \\ \hline 0 \end{array}$
Step 2 Divide 10 by 4. There are 2 left over.	
Step 3 Divide 20 by 4. There is 0 left over.	

Step 1 Divide 6 by 5. There is 1 left over.	$\begin{array}{r} \$1.23 \\ 5\overline{)\$6.15} \\ -5 \\ \hline 1\,1 \\ -1\,0 \\ \hline 15 \\ -15 \\ \hline 0 \end{array}$
Step 2 Divide 11 by 5. There is 1 left over.	
Step 3 Divide 15 by 5. There is 0 left over.	

Divide.

1. $2\overline{)\$3.14}$ 2. $4\overline{)\$6.28}$ 3. $8\overline{)\$9.84}$ 4. $7\overline{)\$7.84}$

5. $5\overline{)\$4.55}$ 6. $3\overline{)\$3.72}$ 7. $4\overline{)\$9.08}$ 8. $2\overline{)\$2.38}$

9. $4\overline{)\$12.84}$ 10. $5\overline{)\$18.80}$ 11. $3\overline{)\$12.42}$ 12. $6\overline{)\$13.44}$

13. $3\overline{)\$16.20}$ 14. $9\overline{)\$46.08}$ 15. $6\overline{)\$17.40}$ 16. $2\overline{)\$18.32}$

Name _____   Date _____

Identify Polygons

Polygons have sides and angles.

	Some Polygons	Sides	Angles
	square	4	4
	triangle	3	3
	rectangle	4	4
	pentagon	5	5
	hexagon	6	6
	octagon	8	8

An octagon has 8 sides and 8 angles.

Name the figure. Write the number of sides and angles.

1.

_____
_____ sides
_____ angles

2.

_____
_____ sides
_____ angles

3.

_____
_____ sides
_____ angles

4.

_____
_____ sides
_____ angles

5.

_____
_____ sides
_____ angles

6.

_____
_____ sides
_____ angles

Name _____   Date _____

Identify Parts of a Circle

Identify each of the parts of a circle.

Center middle of the circle
Radius line segment connecting the center
and a point on the circle
Diameter line segment connecting points
on the circle that passes through
the center of the circle
Chord line segment joining two parts of
the circle

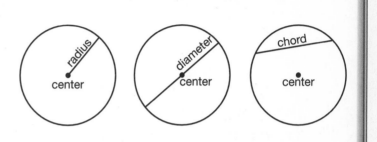

Write the letter to identify each part of the circle.

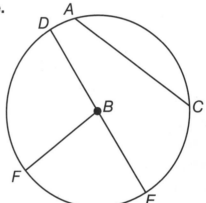

1. center   _____

2. radius   _____

3. diameter   _____

4. chord   _____

Find the radius.

5. diameter = 12 cm   _____   6. diameter = 10 in.   _____

7. diameter = 8 in.   _____   8. diameter = 18 cm   _____

9. diameter = 16 cm   _____   10. diameter = 14 cm   _____

Find the diameter.

11. radius = 7 cm   _____   12. radius = 8 in.   _____

13. radius = 9 in.   _____   14. radius = 6 cm   _____

15. radius = 5 cm   _____   16. radius = 10 cm   _____

Name _____   Date _____

Finding Perimeter or Area

Find perimeter and area of polygons.

Perimeter is the distance around an object. 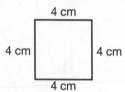 4 cm + 4 cm + 4 cm + 4 cm = 16 cm The perimeter is 16 cm.	**Area** is the number of square units it takes to cover a figure. 3 units × 2 units = 6 square units The area is 6 square units.

Find the perimeter.

1.
3 in.
3 in. 3 in.
3 in.

_____

2.

3 m   3 m

_____

3.
2 cm
2 cm   2 cm
2 cm   2 cm
2 cm

_____

4.
3 cm
6 cm   6 cm
8 cm

_____

Find the area.

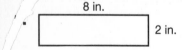
8 in.
2 in.

_____

6.
7 cm
7 cm

_____

Name _____   Date _____

Solid Figures

Identify the faces, edges, and vertices of a prism.

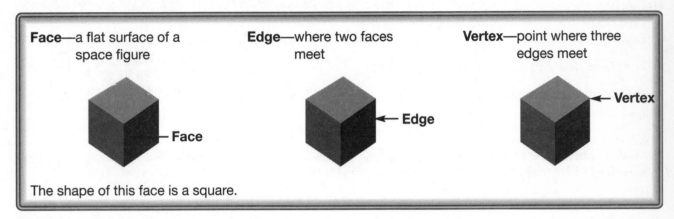

Face—a flat surface of a space figure

Edge—where two faces meet

Vertex—point where three edges meet

← **Vertex**

← **Edge**

— **Face**

The shape of this face is a square.

Write the number of edges and vertices. Identify the shape of the face the arrow points to.

1.

_____

_____ edges

_____ vertices

2.

_____

_____ edges

_____ vertices

3.

_____

_____ edges

_____ vertices

4.

_____

_____ edges

_____ vertices

Name _____ Date _____

Fractions with a Denominator of 100

An equivalent fraction names equal parts.

> **Equivalent Fractions**
>
> The fractions $\frac{1}{2}$ and $\frac{50}{100}$ are equivalent fractions.
>
> Equivalent fractions name equal parts of a region or set.
>
> $\frac{1}{2} = \frac{50}{100}$
>
>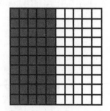

Write the equivalent fraction with a denominator of 100.

1.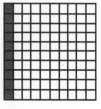

$\frac{1}{4} =$ _____

2.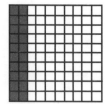

$\frac{3}{4} =$ _____

3.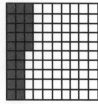

$\frac{1}{10} =$ _____

4.

$\frac{1}{5} =$ _____

5.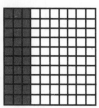

$\frac{3}{10} =$ _____

6.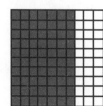

$\frac{7}{10} =$ _____

Name _____ Date _____

Write a Decimal as a Fraction

A part of a region or set can be written as a decimal or a fraction.

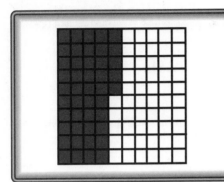

Write a fraction.

$\frac{45}{100}$

Write a decimal.

0.45

Write the decimal as a fraction with a denominator of 100.

1. 0.25 _____

2. 0.03 _____

3. 0.66 _____

4. 0.02 _____

5. 0.98 _____

6. 0.81 _____

7. 0.43 _____

8. 0.23 _____

9. 0.61 _____

10. 0.09 _____

11. 0.14 _____

12. 0.55 _____

13. 0.73 _____

14. 0.78 _____

15. 0.01 _____

16. 0.30 _____

17. 0.84 _____

18. 0.62 _____

Name _____   Date _____

Decimals on a Number Line

Decimals can be shown on a number line.

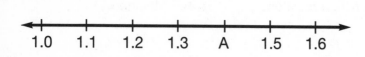

A = 1.4

Write the missing decimals.

1.

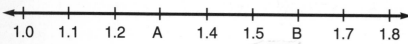

1.0   1.1   1.2   A   1.4   1.5   B   1.7   1.8

A = _____

B = _____

2.

2.4   2.5   A   2.7   2.8   B   3.0   3.1   3.2

A = _____

B = _____

3.

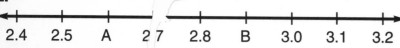

1.9   A   2.1   2.2   2.3   B   2.5   2.6   2.7

A = _____

B = _____

4.

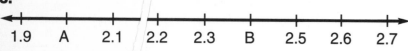

4.1   4.2   A   4.4   4.5   4.6   B   4.8   4.9

A = _____

B = _____

5.

4.9   A   5.1   5.2   5.3   B   5.5   5.6   5.7

A = _____

B = _____

6.

7.1   A   7.3   7.4   B   7.6   7.7   7.8   7.9

A = _____

B = _____

Name _____   Date _____

Compare Fractions and Decimals

Compare fractions and decimals.

Compare $\frac{2}{5}$, $\frac{4}{10}$, and 0.40.

$\frac{2}{5} = \frac{4}{10} = 0.40$

Write each decimal as a fraction. Then write the one that is greater.

1. $\frac{1}{10}$ 0.25   _____

2. $\frac{4}{5}$ 0.65   _____

3. $\frac{3}{10}$ 0.45   _____

4. $\frac{1}{4}$ 0.15   _____

5. $\frac{40}{100}$ 0.45   _____

Write each fraction as a decimal. Then write the one that is greater.

6. $\frac{55}{100}$ 0.61   _____

7. $\frac{1}{4}$ 0.30   _____

8. $\frac{3}{10}$ 0.45   _____

9. $\frac{1}{2}$ 0.27   _____

10. $\frac{4}{10}$ 0.35   _____

Name _____   Date _____

Order Fractions and Decimals

Order fractions and decimals.

> **Write as decimals.**
>
> $\frac{5}{10} = 0.5$ $\frac{1}{4} = 0.25$ $\frac{8}{10} = 0.8$ $\frac{40}{100} = 0.40$
>
> **Order from least to greatest.**
>
> 0.25   0.40   0.5   0.8

Write in order from least to greatest.

1. $\frac{1}{4}$, $\frac{1}{10}$, 0.30   _____

2. 0.50, $\frac{40}{100}$, 0.60   _____

3. $\frac{3}{100}$, 0.25, 0.22   _____

4. $\frac{1}{2}$, 0.55, $\frac{45}{100}$ _____

5. $\frac{60}{100}$, $\frac{7}{10}$, 0.75   _____

Write in order from greatest to least.

6. 0.67, $\frac{6}{10}$, $\frac{75}{100}$ _____

7. 0.27, $\frac{1}{4}$, 0.31   _____

8. $\frac{15}{100}$, 0.16, $\frac{2}{10}$ _____

9. 0.49, $\frac{4}{10}$, 0.45   _____

10. $\frac{60}{100}$, $\frac{1}{2}$, 0.51   _____

Name _____ Date _____

Ordered Pairs and Points

An ordered pair of numbers tells where a point is located.

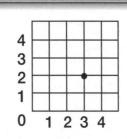

The point is located at (3, 2).

Write the ordered pair for the location.

1. *A* _____

2. *D* _____

3. *E* _____

4. *B* _____

5. *G* _____

6. *I* _____

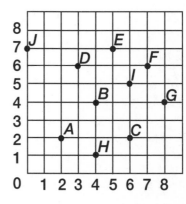

What letter is located at the point named by the ordered pair?

7. (6, 2) _____   **8.** (7, 6) _____

9. (0, 7) _____   **10.** (4, 1) _____

Name _____ Date _____

Plot Points

To write an ordered pair for a point, count the spaces to the right. Then count up.

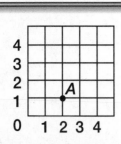

Point *A* is located at (2, 1).

Write the letter at the point for the ordered pair.

1. (2, 3) _____

2. (7, 2) _____

3. (2, 4) _____

4. (6, 5) _____

5. (6, 3) _____

6. (8, 7) _____

7. (4,) _____

8. (, 7) _____

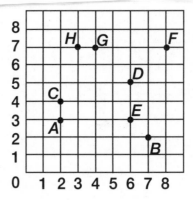

Choose a point for these letters. Write the ordered pair.

9. I _____   **10.** J _____